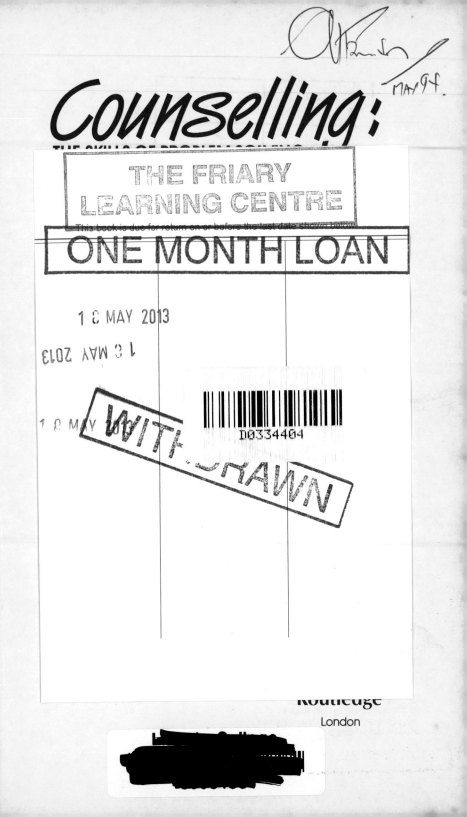

Counselling:

THE SKILLS OF PROBLEM SOLVING

Routledge

London

First published 1989
by Longman Paul Limited
182-190 Wairau Road, Auckland 10,
New Zealand

© 1988 Longman Paul
Published in the UK
by Routledge
11 New Fetter Lane, London, EC4P 4EE
Reprinted 1990, 1991

ISBN 0 415 03956 8

Produced by Longman Paul Limited
Designed by Derek Ward
Cover design by Polly Faulks
Typeset in 10/11 pt Optima Roman
Printed in Hong Kong

Contents

PREFACE   vii

1 INTRODUCTION   1
Values   4
Confidentiality   9
Physical contact   10
Power in counselling   10
Theory and practice   13
The problem-solving model   16

2 THE COUNSELLOR IS A PERSON   17
The counsellor's needs in counselling   19
The counsellor's personal cultural history   21
Developing self-awareness   22
The counsellor's personal qualities   25
Role-playing as a counselling skill   27

**3 BEGINNING THE PROBLEM-SOLVING
PROCESS**   30
Introduction   30
Problem definition   31
Goal setting   31
Strategy selection   32
Implementation of strategy   32
Evaluation   33
The skills of problem definition   33
Getting started   33
Is the client voluntary or involuntary?   34

What background information is available and how much
   is needed? 35
The counsellor's preferences 36
Availability of information 36
Types of information 36
The first sighting and meeting 37
Self-awareness 38
Open invitation to talk 42
Sorting issues 43
Open and closed questions 44
Topic following 45
Minimal encouragers 46
Active listening 47
The language of counselling 47
Engaging reluctant clients 51
Thinking aloud 54
Immediacy 55
Using silence 55
Identifying feelings 56
Expressing feelings 57
Reflection 60
Accurate understanding 61

**4 DEVELOPING THE PROBLEM-SOLVING
PROCESS** 64
The skills of goal setting 64
Direct questioning 64
Dealing with discrepancies 65
Setting goals 66
Supporting and encouraging 67
Interpretation 68
Giving information 69
Giving advice 70
Influencing 71
Giving directions 71
Using personal examples 72
Advising a delay 72
Gaining commitment 73
The skills of strategy selection 75
Anticipating situations 75
Providing models 75
Role-playing 77
Using rewards 78

**5 COMPLETING THE PROBLEM-SOLVING
  PROCESS**   82
  The skills of implementing strategies   82
    Making records   82
    Bodily awareness, relaxation, activities   83
    Thoughts and imagery   86
    Desensitisation   88
    Mixing strategies   89
    Homework   90
  The skills of evaluation   91
    Assessing results   91
    Summarising   91
    Generalising   92
    Referral   93
    Termination   94

**6 NGA MATAPIHI O TE WAIORA
  (WINDOWS ON MĀORI WELL-BEING)**   97

7 FAMILY COUNSELLING   107
  Family organisation   107
  Stages of family counselling   112
    1. The referral   112
    2. Introduction, greetings   113
    3. Structuring time   114
    4. Problem definition   115
    5. Solutions   117
    6. Therapeutic suggestions or homework   119
    7. Terminating   120
  Brief family counselling   121

8 CONSULTATION   124
  Introduction   124
  Types of consultation   125
    Providing an expert service   125
    Prescribing a remedy   125
    Mediating   126
    Collaborating   126
  The consultation process   126
  Elaboration of the consultation process   128
    Preparation   128
    Making contact   128
    Diagnosing problems   129

Gathering information 129
Setting goals and objectives 130
Choosing a solution 131
Acquiring resources 131
Carrying out interventions 131
Evaluating 132
Terminating 132
Dealing with resistance 133
Effectiveness of consultation 133
Questions to ask when choosing a consultant 133
An example of a consultation 134
The counsellor-consultant as trainer 135
Clarity of aims and objectives 135
Size and composition of groups 136
Voluntary or involuntary membership 137
The physical setting 138
Timing and length of course 138
Materials 138
Leaders of training courses and workshops 139
Leading groups 140
Sample course 142

9 DEVELOPING COMPETENCE 144
Integrating the skills 144
Estimating progress 145
Evaluating effectiveness 146
Supervision 147
  What is supervision? 147
  Who benefits from supervision? 147
  Who should supervise? 148
  How does one find a supervisor who will meet one's
  needs? 148
  Where should supervision take place? 149
  How often and how long? 149
  How is supervision carried out? 150
  Should audio or video tape recordings be used? 152
  How is a supervision relationship terminated? 152
Managing stress and preventing burnout 152
Continuing your learning 154

ANSWERS TO EXERCISES 155

REFERENCES 159

SELECT BIBLIOGRAPHY 160

Preface

This book expresses our belief that counselling, the process of helping others, can be described as a series of skills within a problem-solving format that is governed by some important ethical principles. We believe too, that this view of counselling and these skills, stages, and principles are of general value and that they should be more widely known and practised.

Counselling: The Skills of Problem-Solving has been written with a minimum of technical terms, and is intended for counsellors working in various settings (educational, vocational, medical, social, and rehabilitative) and for those offering training courses for such counsellors.

In some chapters the counsellor is consistently referred to as 'he' and the client as 'she'. In others this pattern is reversed. This was done both to simplify the presentation within chapters and to express our commitment to the equality of the sexes.

Each of the authors has shared equally in writing the book and thus each accepts equal responsibility for its contents. The order of authorship does not indicate any difference in contributions. Collectively we have been able to draw upon many years of experience in counselling research and in the study, teaching, and practice of counselling, mainly in New Zealand, but also in Australia, England, and the United States. Each of us has been enriched by the sharing of these experiences with our teachers, colleagues, students, and clients. To all these people we are very grateful. In particular we wish to acknowledge the contribution of Hinekahukura Barrett-Aranui. Her chapter, Windows on Māori Well-Being, adds an important cultural perspective.

Anne Munro
Bob Manthei
John Small

1

Introduction

Counselling, along with the many other ways of helping people, is becoming increasingly profession- alised. As this happens, there is a need to show how, with training and practice, it can be performed better. This is a challenging task, and this book does not claim to cover all aspects of counselling. Its main contri- bution is to show how people can be helped by using certain practical skills within a framework of problem- solving.

Effective counselling requires much more than the practice of particular verbal skills: counsellors need to know themselves well, they need to know other people from study and experience, they need to know a good deal about social institutions and their influ- ences, and they need realistic knowledge about the forces in society which create advantages and disadvantages – the market- place, racism, sexism, and similar forms of prejudice. Power and status issues underlie most of society's problems, and as discussed below they are also present within counselling relationships no matter how much counsellors may want to eliminate them. This book does not deal directly with all of these important topics, but no one should feel competent as a counsellor without some knowledge of them. Nor does the book address the important problem of the specialised knowledge that is expected of most counsellors, depending on where the counsellor works – in a school, in a government department, in a hospital, in a child-care centre, or any other place.

The book's focus is on giving beginning counsellors a structure for dealing with problems as they are presented that is neither too loose nor too restrictive, and within that structure a variety of skills which can be used according to the counsellor's purpose at any particular time. These central features – a problem-solving approach and a range of verbal skills – appear in Chapters Three, Four, and Five. They are preceded in Chapter Two by discussions and exercises on counsellors' self-knowledge.

An emphasis is placed on describing skills and giving ideas and suggestions that can be readily learnt and put into practice by a wide variety of people. While skills and knowledge from social sciences lie behind much of the book, it is not necessary for those who wish to become effective counsellors to have undertaken academic courses. For this reason it is the practical applications of theory and research, combined with our accumulated experience as teachers, counsellors, and supervisors that we have translated for the benefit of the growing numbers of people who wish to become effective counsellors.

The purpose of this book is to describe how people can improve their methods of helping others solve their problems. Successful problem-solving should lead to better self-understanding and an increased ability to solve other problems in the future. The term 'counselling' is used here to cover the various skills and principles of helping people to do these things. The setting within which these skills and principles are described is a face-to-face relationship between two people – counsellor and client. However the essentials of individual counselling (sometimes called casework) are directly applicable in other settings as well. These include consultation and training, family counselling, and various kinds of group work, along with aspects of social work, teaching, supervision, and administration.

It is useful to consider at the outset some of the ways in which counselling relationships differ from ordinary social interactions between friends, acquaintances, and colleagues. There are of course many similarities, but in counselling certain features are evident in greater degree. People start to become clients when they invite help or begin to express their concerns to another who is willing to listen and to help them to find a solution, using interpersonal skills of the kinds described in this book. Many of these skills are not peculiar to counselling, but the relationship in which they occur approximates counselling when, in addition, the relationship is voluntary, there is a high degree of confidentiality, and there is an agreement on the personal responsibility of the client. Moreover, counsellors do not allow their counselling relationships to be compromised by any other relationships they might have with their clients, for example as friend, or as administrative supervisor. The more of these features that are apparent in a social relationship, and the more clearly they are evident, the more appropriate it is to regard it as counselling. A relationship that lacks several of these features or shows them to only a weak extent will not be effective counselling, even if it seems to be counselling in a formal sense, because, for example, it takes place in a counsellor's office by appointment.

Like related activities such as teaching, administering, or leading others, the ability to counsel may seem somewhat mysterious. But it should not be regarded as a mystique or special charisma bestowed on only a few individuals. It is true that some people are effective counsellors without having studied counselling systematically. They seem to have an intuitive knack for saying and doing the most helpful thing at the right time, and to have personal attributes that enhance their effectiveness. A good deal remains to be learnt about this, but enough progress has been made in studying and teaching the counselling process to justify confidence in describing it as separate skills used within a certain kind of relationship for the purpose of problem-solving. If counselling is to be demystified and made more widely available to clients and to counsellors, the first step is to describe its component skills in language that is both clear and non-technical.

This is a central point. There are many possible views of the counselling process, but for learning and teaching purposes it is particularly useful to view it as a series of interactions within an authentic relationship, consisting of certain behaviours by one person which partly influence the way the other person responds. What the counsellor says usually has some effect on what the client says, and vice versa. This perspective is not intended to diminish the importance of qualitative factors such as the degree of empathy shown by the counsellor. These factors are extremely important in counselling, and it is essential that beginners become highly sensitive to them. This book deals with these matters, but its main focus is on separate interactions and their effects within a problem-solving model.

Effective counsellors use different skills at different times according to what seems to be most helpful. In the early stages of counselling when one is trying to get a clear view of the problem, it is usually best to listen carefully and to respond to clients' overt behaviours and apparent needs. At other times influencing clients by getting them to do something may be much more appropriate. As an example, sometimes counsellors will purposely ignore obvious signs of anxiety in a client. At other times they may simply comment upon them openly but neutrally, and say no more about them, thus indicating an acceptance of the behaviour. Alternatively, they may decide to reduce the anxiety level so that a freer discussion can take place. Whatever is decided, counsellors must not only be aware of the likely consequences of such variations but also have the skills to carry out their intentions. Exactly what the counsellor decides to do is of course a personal and professional decision – a function of training, experience, and knowledge.

In another important sense, however, the primary role of the counsellor is not that of merely using certain techniques, even with warmth and sympathy. Counselling is essentially an ethical task: it is to serve the client's best interests. These can be difficult to determine, but the role of servant is central to counselling, for the counsellor's ultimate responsibility is to empower people, to help them to get what they want, provided that this does not conflict with the counsellor's personal values.

Many people become counsellors because they want to work with people in these ways. But if clients show clearly that they do not want help and do not wish to change – for whatever reason – then counsellors have no right to impose their views or use their skills, regardless of their expertise, insights, or their ability to predict outcomes. Behind this assertion lies an awareness that sometimes the counsellor's need to give help may be as strong as, or even stronger than, the client's need to receive it. As will be discussed in Chapter Two, counsellors must be knowledgeable not only about others but also about themselves.

VALUES

Values may be thought of as the 'oughts', the ideals on which decisions are based. They are an indispensable part of reality. All individuals behave in accordance with a set of values, whether these have been thought out and made explicit or not. Therefore, a counsellor cannot maintain a position of neutrality.

Counsellors will be concerned with four types of values: moral, social, legal, and spiritual. Moral values are concerned with concepts of good and evil and often find expression in social values. We may subscribe to the idea that love is good and express this socially in upholding the institutions of marriage and the family. The law may then support these values by regarding marriage as a legal contract, not to be broken easily, and by protecting children through laws relating to custody and maintenance. When these values are placed in a larger context, such as consideration of the meaning and purpose of life, the spiritual dimension exists.

Again, counsellors will be involved in value questions of varying levels of importance. Respect for life is a high-level value, while conventions of dress and housekeeping are not so vital ultimately, although some people behave as if they were.

Are there any basic values to which society can expect counsellors to subscribe? In the section on the counsellor's personal qualities in Chapter Two, a number of desirable counsellor characteristics are suggested, among them acceptance of others, open-mindedness, respect for others, self-awareness and objectivity. It is reasonable to assume that underlying such qualities are the basic values of tolerance, concern for others, recognition of the worth of each individual, belief in oneself, honesty, truthfulness, goodwill, and caring. These values are widely accepted as essential to community life, and, because of its nature, the counselling relationship demands that counsellors hold these values.

In an increasingly divergent society the counsellor may find himself at variance in values and lifestyle with some of his clients and with sections of the community, particularly on controversial issues such as sexual behaviour, contraception, abortion, drug use, energy conservation, and attitudes towards racial and gender differences.

The counsellor usually works within institutional limitations. Each agency, preferably explicitly, but sometimes only implicitly, has its boundaries within which the counsellor is expected to function. A church counselling agency may insist that its counsellors be committed Christians and that the spiritual dimension be an essential part of any counselling. A school may insist on the right of parents to know that their children are receiving counselling and may place age limits on certain types of counselling, especially where there are laws to consider, as in the matter of discussing contraception with students under a certain age.

Often then, the counsellor is placed in situations of value conflict. Values are part of his own identity and he must expect to meet clients from other cultures and subcultures who hold very different values. Differences in age, race, sex, and socio-economic status increase the likelihood of value conflicts. For example, a counsellor may believe that open sharing of feelings, respecting the rights of others, and talking through disagreements are the best ways of working through a conflict. His client, however, may live in a setting where physical violence is the usual method of settling arguments and anything else is regarded as soft.

Society's expectations of the counsellor's role, especially in the counselling of juveniles, may cause value conflicts for a counsellor. What of the counsellor facing a 16-year-old school girl who is living with a 32-year-old separated father of two? The client's concern may be to cope with the stresses associated with this situation while choosing to remain in it, but the parents', the school's and society's expectation probably would be that the counsellor would attempt to persuade the girl to terminate this relationship.

A third value conflict situation is the one already implicit in the counsellor's placement within an agency which has certain boundaries to its role, especially if it is a state agency. Where a social worker is investigating an adoption or fostering placement, she may be convinced of the personal qualities of the prospective parents but their home may not meet the physical criteria. A school often expects guidance counsellors to persuade academically able pupils who are resistant to attending university to change their minds.

Where there are inconsistencies among a client's values, the counsellor's role is clearer: he should confront the client with the inconsistencies, and thus help her to clarify her values. However, this can still be difficult. A very aggressive client may appear to value her child's well-being in seeking help with his management but may then, by refusing to co-operate, reveal her true position which is rejecting of him. It takes courage to confront such a client with her true values. If this is done, it might then even be necessary for the counsellor to withdraw from the case.

The counsellor may also meet clients who have contravened society's standards or broken laws. There can then be a conflict between the counsellor's duty to his client and his duty to society, especially where serious crimes are revealed, eg, serious drug offences, extensive theft, hit-and-run driving or even murder. How then can the counsellor cope with the value conflicts that will be an inevitable part of his work?

It is not possible to give specific directions but the following general guidelines can help.

1 Each person has the right to follow his or her own conscience.
2 To remain true to himself the counsellor cannot divorce himself from his own social, moral, and spiritual values. He has a right to them. But he must know himself, recognise his values and be honest about them.
3 His task is to help the client rationally examine her values,

make her own decisions (preferably avoiding harmful extremes), and establish her own identity.

4 Young people are particularly quick to see through phoney values and to challenge double standards. The counsellor should honestly recognise the justice of some allegations by clients rather than defend the institution and his colleagues automatically. It may be possible to teach the client appropriate ways of challenging the system.

5 The counsellor does not have the right to impose his own values on clients.

6 His position is not that of judge: his function is not to assign guilt or innocence but to encourage objective evaluation of attitudes, standards, and actions.

7 Many clients have an expectation and fear of being judged. They already feel guilty because of having contravened their own, their family's, or society's moral code. It does not help to deny the reality of this conflict by suggesting that there is no need to regard their behaviour as deviant.

8 A counsellor does not operate in isolation. He is usually a type of social agent, expected to work within the law and basic values of society. His boundaries may be reasonably narrow and defined by statute as in the case of social workers in a government department, or they may be wide as in the case of detached youth workers. However, at some stage a decision as to how much can be accepted will have to be made.

9 If there is any place for judgement, it should be actions rather than persons that are judged.

There are further ethical values and assumptions that we, the authors, make about counselling which should be made explicit. Firstly, the counselling skills described are confined almost exclusively to influencing people through talking. Such techniques as legal coercion, medication, testing, or the use of apparatus or equipment are sometimes regarded as part of counselling. However, because they raise complex issues about the rights of clients and the authority and qualifications of counsellors, these techniques are beyond the scope of this book.

Secondly, since counselling means dealing with people, the interpersonal skills described are not neutral or value-free in the sense that practical skills are. Counselling of whatever kind is rightly taken to represent a set of beliefs and assumptions about people, about interpersonal relationships, and about ways of influencing others. Among the values and assumptions we hold are the following:

1 Many people need help in coping with their difficulties.
2 Most people who need help have within themselves some resources for coping which counsellors can elicit and strengthen.
3 People usually respond better to counselling when they feel some degree of sincerity, warmth, and empathy towards them.
4 Counselling is based partly upon rational approaches, partly upon the expression of feelings, and partly upon the assessment of values.
5 While counsellors offer a variety of counselling skills within a relationship of caring and sharing, ultimately it is the client who determines the content, the methods, and the success of counselling.
6 Counsellors have a duty to maintain and develop themselves professionally by undergoing supervision.

Thirdly, when a counsellor and his client are from different cultures or are of different genders or social conditioning, such differences will very often have important effects on counselling. Differences in race, gender, and social class are probably the most important factors. However, counselling can be affected by any marked difference between counsellor and client in life experience and world view, such as age, religion, and responsibility for child care.

Another basic issue concerning values is whether in any particular case counselling is in fact the most appropriate way of helping. Instead of encouraging a client to keep making appointments to discuss a problem, the counsellor may be well advised to suggest other means of improvement such as music, drama, physical activity, change of diet, or meditation. It is important that counsellors be open-minded and knowledgeable about such alternatives, and when these seem appropriate, to inform clients about them and encourage them to try them.

Counsellors should recognise, too, that helping one person to change may alter family relationships. For young clients this may result in intolerable pressures being placed on them to continue or resume some former role in the family, such as scapegoat, baby, or symptom carrier. Counsellors should be cautious about trying to alter family patterns, because what is done to one person is likely to affect others. Indeed they should be cautious about suggesting any new behaviours because, to many clients, a counsellor's values will represent positions on, for example, morality or religion with which clients disagree fundamentally. It is possible for a forceful counsellor inadvertently to influence clients to accept something they really do not desire.

As well, many counsellors aspire to high levels of personal functioning which others may not want, nor be able to reach. In making suggestions for change, a counsellor may be asking a client to cope with tremendous mental pain. In a sense the process resembles an operation. Adults have the right to choose to accept or reject surgery after the situation has been explained to them. Clients seeking counselling should have a similar right.

The key considerations in deciding whether to counsel or not, and if so how to weigh up the values at stake, are the welfare and rights of the client, including her values and those of significant others. Clients' wishes are paramount, but if they are juveniles or if their lives or their physical health are at risk, it may be necessary to overrule their wishes.

CONFIDENTIALITY

The client's right to confidentiality is regarded as basic because the counselling relationship is an intimate one based on trust. Confidentiality means keeping secret any information concerning the client which she has revealed in counselling. Unfortunately, absolute confidentiality is probably rare because of human fallibility, staff discussions, and inter-agency sharing, or client permission to divulge information.

Most clients divulge information about their situations, their past, and their innermost feelings in the belief that they are sharing confidences, because this is necessary if help is to be obtained. They trust the counsellor with such information, assuming it will remain confidential. Within limits, confidences must be respected.

We suggest the following guidelines:

1 The client should know where she stands in relation to confidentiality. For example, if case discussion is routine within an agency, the client should be told this.
2 Where referral to another agency or consultation with another family member seems appropriate, the client's prior permission should be sought.
3 When a client specifically requests confidentiality regarding a particular disclosure, this must be respected.
4 Where confidentiality has to be broken because of the law or because of danger to the client's life, she should be informed as soon as possible.

5 Records of interviews should be minimal, noting only what is essential within the particular agency setting. Records should be locked up, shared only with authorised recipients who would also be bound by confidentiality, and destroyed when the counselling relationship is terminated.

6 An atmosphere of confidentiality is even more important than any verbal assurances of it. If, for example, during the interview notetaking is considered essential, the counsellor could offer to let the client see what is being written or even write it herself. Confidentiality then takes on a new meaning for her.

7 Confidentiality, when part of a professional code of ethics, should be upheld.

PHYSICAL CONTACT

Another ethical question relates to physical contact between counsellor and client. Some counsellors say that they sometimes hold a client's hand, or put an arm around a client's shoulder, or even embrace a client. The question is whether such behaviour is ethically and professionally justified as a means of helping clients.

Physical contact between counsellor and client is more acceptable in some institutions, such as hospitals, than in others, such as schools. Even within an institution it is more justified in some situations than in others, such as an interview resulting in much emotional upset compared with one involving only rational discussion. Finally, in some counsellor-client pairings physical contact seems to be more accepted than others, for example a female counsellor with a female client compared with a male counsellor with a female client. Although norms are changing, female counsellors may still be seen more naturally and effectively to initiate such contacts with both males and females.

In many circumstances a client may well be helped towards solving her problems (the purpose of counselling) by physical contact with her counsellor. On the other hand, there is still something of a risk in physical contact in non-medical settings. The following may be the crucial question: when the issue of physical contact arises, how will the client's needs be served by such contact?

POWER IN COUNSELLING

The term power as used here refers to the ways in which, and the extent to which, influence or ascendancy of one person over another is gained and maintained. Some interpersonal power is sanctioned by law (eg, parents over children, teachers over students); some is a consequence of social conventions and conditioning (eg, older people over younger people); and some is achieved by psychological or social means (eg, asking questions in certain ways, acquiring status symbols). It is possible to see interpersonal power as a factor or at least a potential issue in virtually every social relationship, including counselling.

Power relationships in counselling are unequal from the outset. Merely asking another to help confers power on that person. The client, in confessing her need, makes herself vulnerable. It is the task of the counsellor to empower the client so that she can overcome the feelings of being stuck and unable to change. By the same token, the counsellor needs to appreciate the fact that he is empowered by the client when she takes the risk of opening herself to him.

This inherent inequality in the relationship is usually enlarged when there are ethnic, gender, or other important differences between the counsellor and the client. In our society men hold the reins of power in all important spheres of life, and despite some recent changes, statistics still support those who view women as inferior to men. Women's principal occupations — housekeepers, care-givers, nurturers, and assistants to people in high-status jobs — are generally devalued, as shown by the fact that they often are given either no wages at all or at best a very low wage for the work that they do. Minority ethnic groups are also accorded inferior social status, their values often being considered naive and ill-judged in a materialistic world.

Therefore, if a woman goes to a male counsellor, or a Maori or Samoan to a European counsellor, the inequality that is inherent in the counselling relationship is almost inevitably exacerbated. The differences in power between the sexes and between ethnic groups is so great that one may well want to maintain that counselling should take place only between people of the same sex and the same race. Desirable though that may be, however, it is not always possible, and in any case, regardless of counsellor-client differences, inequality still prevails in every counselling relationship.

What does this mean for a counsellor? Mainly, it means that the counsellor should stay in his role of empowering the client, and resist temptations to use his powers to make the client accept advice, adopt values, and make decisions that she might not want. There could also be a temptation for the counsellor to proceed at a pace that may be inappropriate for the client. To truly empower the client, the counsellor must first recognise that he cannot give help: he can only offer it. He must accept that if power is to remain with the client, she must be left free to choose whether or not to change. True helping depends on choice.

The counsellor may work as part of a team that includes psychologists, social workers, medical personnel, teachers, or managers. It is important that within the team, roles are defined clearly, and that people work within their roles, respecting the roles and the rights of colleagues. Conflicts over power are likely to occur if this is not done.

Some relationships within an organisation will be hierarchical, and the counsellor may be subject to the authority of a person, such as a school principal, who is not trained in counselling and who does not accept typical counsellor values. Acceptance of a position within the organisation presumes acceptance of its authority structure. However, it is not necessary for the counsellor to meekly accept all directives if they are not in accordance with the counsellor's personal or professional values, or if they threaten his authority in his role. The counsellor has the right, and indeed the duty, to state his point of view, and to assert himself in defence of it. He should have been equipped in his training with the skills which enable him to reduce or resolve disagreements and conflicts.

To be seen as authentic within his organisation, the counsellor, in his relationships with his colleagues, should model desirable counselling qualities. That is, he should show warmth, empathy, and respect for others; he should be prepared to disclose himself as a person with strengths and weaknesses; and he should be prepared to listen to other points of view, face conflicts honestly, and where necessary accept workable compromises.

The environment in which counselling takes place often affects the power relationship. Much counsellor training appears to assume that individual counsellor-client contact will occur in an office that is soundproof, private, and pleasantly decorated, and that the time available will be free from interruptions. However, the reality may be very different.

A secondary school guidance counsellor may work in a noisy, publicly situated, poorly-furnished office/storeroom, and be subject to frequent interruptions from the telephone, and from staff and students wanting his attention. These factors underline his comparatively low status in the institution, and because his clients are not adults his status is also lower than that of, say, his colleague who is a counsellor in a tertiary institution. A visiting teacher will often interview people in their homes, perhaps to the accompaniment of the television, the washing machine, or the distractions of pre-school children. Being on someone else's territory, he may need to be more circumspect in his counselling because he could be asked to leave at any time. In the case of telephone counselling there is no face-to-face contact, and this greatly reduces the interpersonal power of the counsellor. In a woman's refuge there may be distressed children or other residents present, which a counsellor may find distracting.

At times counselling takes place in a vehicle en route to home, to the court, or to a hospital. In the intimacy of such a setting some otherwise quiet clients will open up. By contrast, young people in particular may confide in a counsellor during a game of table tennis or some other recreational or practical activity. On the other hand, what might appeal to a counsellor as an ideal office with tasteful prints and calm soft decor may be inhibiting to clients used to less affluent surroundings. Such a setting may serve to emphasise differences in status, and thus make it more difficult for the counsellor to help.

The mere fact of requiring a client to come to the counsellor's territory confers further power on the latter, no matter how well the surroundings may accord with the client's background and values. Almost always she has to adjust to a strange setting which conveys some powerful messages, especially about relative status. On the other hand, a counsellor venturing on to a client's territory – be it a private home, a marae, or a factory canteen – where he is unsupported by the trappings of his own space, has much less power than in his office.

Counsellors should be aware of these issues. If possible, clients should have some choice about the meeting place; certainly they should be made as comfortable as possible in strange surroundings by allowing a little time for them to settle. It may be possible to minimise interruptions from the telephone; a sign could be put on the door; and those who often interrupt could be asked to respect the counsellor's wish for privacy at such times. Where other people, especially small children, are present the counsellor might decide to ask directly for the chance to talk in another room or outside if someone else can supervise the children. Alternatively, the counsellor could have some toys or games to occupy children. He might ask for the radio or television to be switched off or down. However, outside his office the counsellor will often have little option but to try to screen out distractions.

THEORY AND PRACTICE

There are many different theories and special approaches to counselling, but they are beyond the scope of this book. We urge counᴐrs to become thoroughly acquainted with the major ones early ᴗ their training, and to learn the many useful ideas and techniques that have been developed within them. The different theories can provide new perspectives on clients' problems and suggest alternative ways for counsellors to help. Counsellors eventually face the task of developing their own personal style or theory of counselling, but before doing so they should read widely and with discrimination. This will help them to avoid making a premature commitment to any one theory.

It is important to emphasise that so far years of careful comparative studies have failed to show that any one theory or approach is generally superior to any other. There are a number of reasons for this, the main ones being the following:

1 It is extremely difficult and expensive to design studies which would satisfactorily compare even just two theories. The best one that has ever been done (Sloane et al., 1975) found very few important differences in effectiveness between two major approaches.

2 The hope that newer comparative methods such as meta-analysis would show which theories were best has not yet been realised either, as is shown in the summary by Ivey et al. (1987). It should be noted, as Ivey does, that this does not mean that counselling, generally speaking, is ineffective – only that it is very difficult to show that any particular approach is the best.

3 Because of the cross-fertilisation of ideas through journals, training programmes, and professional organisations, it is most unlikely that any theory is now distinctly different from all others in the way it is practised.

4 Individual differences between clients require different approaches, so that unless a counsellor has the power and the desire to screen out all those who do not fit some very distinct theory and technique, some sort of eclecticism seems inevitable.

Besides considering theory from such a perspective, our focus is on theory from more practical points of view – theory in the sense of providing a rationale for whatever model of counselling is adopted, and theory in the sense of thinking about practical issues as they arise in counselling.

We would like to emphasise counselling as a problem-solving activity, within which it is important to distinguish several distinct phases or stages, with characteristic skills at each phase. We commend no particular theory of personality or human development, not because we think such conceptions are unimportant or irrelevant, but because they need whole books to themselves. For much the same reason we make no reference to medical and psychological pathologies, even though it is important that counsellors know something about such matters. Counselling theory here is presented in terms of a general model of problem-solving, in which counsellors are recommended to accept problems as clients present them, and to assume that clients can be helped to understand themselves and their situations better and work out their own solutions. The model does not require extensive investigations into causes and factors from the past, although these may be useful in some circumstances. Nor does it depend upon counsellors being expert at diagnoses and interpretations, although such skills are also useful to have, and counsellors certainly should be constantly considering possible reasons and explanations for things they find puzzling.

Theory in the sense of making decisions while actually engaged in counselling is closely allied to this. When they are talking to clients, counsellors are often processing many different kinds of knowledge at once and considering their possible relevance in the case. The counsellor may be wondering, for example, about how well he is communicating with the client and vice versa, what sorts of approaches might be best to try first, the counsellor's own personal, subjective reaction to the client and what she is saying, the possible impact on the client of some life crisis that has been mentioned. Counsellors frequently deal with several of these sorts of issues at the same time, and it is the pressure of doing so for long periods that contributes much to counsellor stress. But there is no way of counselling effectively which does not involve constant self-questioning and thinking about the process. Acquiring the habit of thinking about counselling as problematic in these ways, and talking the problems over with a supervisor, is a way of developing a personal theory of counselling. This sort of counselling theory is every bit as important, in fact usually more so, than the theoretical knowledge that is gained only from reading.

In short, we strongly recommend that counsellors become familiar with the major theories of counselling, and take from them those features that seem to be most useful. But counsellors also need to develop some sort of practical model to guide their day-to-day work, and for this we recommend a problem-solving, skills-based model. We also recommend that counsellors acquire the habit of self-questioning even while engaged in listening and responding to their clients. The aim should be to integrate various theoretical and practical considerations, together with one's own unique pattern of values and experiences, into a personal theory of counselling.

THE PROBLEM-SOLVING MODEL

The problem-solving model of counselling does not differ in its essentials from approaches to the solving of problems that have been found useful in other contexts. Indeed, it is because of the wide applicability of problem-solving models that this approach to counselling is strongly commended here. It serves as a useful practical guide for a beginning counsellor, giving a positive, goal-oriented framework which can provide structure but still allow the counsellor a good deal of freedom to choose from a range of styles and techniques.

Of the various models of problem-solving that have been proposed for counselling, the five-step approach of Dixon and Glover (1984) is simple and useful. Their approach, which is used in this book, involves: (1) problem definition; (2) goal selection; (3) strategy selection; (4) implementation of strategy; and (5) evaluation. The exact number of steps and their precise content are not important: the main thing for counsellors to recognise is the value of being reasonably systematic and for them to see in the scheme a good decision-making process.

Counsellors should realise that different clients will have difficulties at different stages of the problem-solving process. For some it will be that they find it hard to pin down their concerns and state them in the form of a problem, while for others it may seem impossible to think up alternative ways of acting. Counsellors have to work harder at those steps of the process that clients find most difficult to handle. It is important that counsellors make sure that all the main stages of the process are followed, and thus be ready on occasions to go back to an earlier stage (eg, problem definition) when it becomes evident that this has not been fully dealt with.

Another important point about adopting a problem-solving approach to counselling is that it can be used to teach clients a general coping skill which can be transferred to other situations besides the particular concern that was brought to the counsellor in the first place. Counsellors should therefore emphasise their roles as guides within a process. This can be done by making sure that the process is clear to their clients, by putting as much responsibility as possible on to their clients, and by spending time at the end of the session discussing what has been learnt and considering how the procedure might be applied in other situations.

2

The counsellor is a person

In any interpersonal situation, whether group or individual, in which one person assumes the role of 'counsellor', that person also assumes a responsibility for her own behaviour, her knowledge of herself, and her ability to relate effectively to another. Anyone who undertakes to be a counsellor must be prepared to interact as a real person with the client and to strive for an awareness of the factors involved in the process. As it is impossible for a counsellor to be totally objective and rational, anyone who strives to be so denies herself a most valuable source of counselling information – her own feelings, perceptions, hunches, and ideas.

Maximum use must be made of all sources of counselling information. This means that the counsellor must rely not only on her perceptions of and understanding of the client's situation as it is related to her, but also on her own feelings about and reactions to what is happening at the time. This latter source is often purposely ignored because it is thought that subjective impressions are necessarily inaccurate and biased. They are, however, potentially the more accurate of the two types of information, provided the counsellor can develop her self-awareness to a level that will enable her accurately to identify and interpret her own reactions and feelings. By contrast, her understanding of another person's situation is always diminished by the fact that any communication from one person to another is prone to some degree of distortion and error. Counselling can be thought of as a dynamic relationship involving two people, and one in which the counsellor's knowledge of herself is as important as the knowledge of the client and of counselling principles.

This dynamic relationship is a process of defining and redefining the specific roles that the counsellor and client will play. Participants can decide *how* to respond to one another, but not *whether* they will respond. For example, in any encounter with another person, everything said or done communicates to the other person how one is willing to relate. If someone says, 'I don't understand what we are supposed to be doing', any response (verbal or non-verbal) by another person begins to define a relationship between them. How would each of these responses to the statement above begin to define a relationship?

1 'I don't either. Let's ask someone else.'
2 'Maybe you should listen more.'
3 'I don't either. What should we do?'
4 Shrug of the shoulders.
5 Say nothing, merely turn away from the person.
6 'Let me see if I can find out for you, OK?'
7 'We are supposed to be reading pages 46–52.'

In the first example, the respondent refuses to assume a leadership or information-giver's role and instead becomes an equal by admitting her ignorance and suggesting that both ask someone else. In the second example, a critical, distant position is assumed that clearly indicates the respondent does not want the speaker to become dependent on her in any way. In (3), after admitting she does not know, the respondent refuses to accept a leadership role and instead tries to get the speaker to take over or at least recognise that they both have some responsibility for solving the problem. The shrug will probably be interpreted as, 'Don't ask me; I don't want to get involved', indicating a desire for no further interaction. The action in (5), no matter how it is done, clearly indicates the respondent's desire for non-involvement. Example (6) illustrates the respondent's willingness to accept a supportive leadership role. The final example gives the information required but probably leaves the speaker undecided about whether further interaction can occur.

This same process of defining and redefining a relationship occurs in counselling. Every word, gesture, and silence alters how the counsellor and client will relate while together.

THE COUNSELLOR'S NEEDS IN COUNSELLING

Before seriously considering herself a counsellor, each person should critically and honestly examine her own motivations for taking on the responsibilities of helping another person. Very simply, she should ask herself: 'What do I expect from the relationship? What will be my satisfactions and rewards in helping others?'

A counsellor's reasons for helping are seldom entirely pure and altruistic, but every counsellor should be open to and aware of her motivations. After all, these motivations can profoundly influence her effectiveness. The counsellor who helps others in order to avoid dealing with her own problems will be limited in her effectiveness. Even if clients do not 'see through' her in a completely accurate way, they will never develop the confidence and trust in her that is essential if she is to help them effectively. Similarly, the counsellor who encourages her clients to confide in her because it gives her status and control will soon find that she will have only one type of client, as others will avoid her and her controlling behaviour.

Some counsellors may desire close contact with others but be unable to achieve these relationships in normal interpersonal situations. By becoming counsellors they are able to avoid facing up to their own deficiencies and to feel competent and fulfilled in working closely with others. There are other counsellors who firmly believe they have answers to life's problems that should be shared with others. With the best of intentions they try to convert clients to their way of thinking but end up alienating many. Others counsel out of a sincere wish to help, with no other hidden motivation. Very often they are unaware of their own rewards and satisfactions. They may be viewed with some scepticism and distrust by the more suspicious or cynical client. Whatever the reasons for helping others, the counsellor's credibility and, hence, her effectiveness will be enhanced by her awareness and acceptance of those reasons.

The first reasons that come to mind might not always be the most honest or accurate. Self-deception in this area hinders effectiveness and, as suggested earlier, *real* motives will be quickly perceived by clients. Adolescents are particularly quick to 'see through' the phoney adult or the counsellor who is only enforcing the school rules in a 'softer' way. Discovering her needs and motivations involves the counsellor in an ongoing examination of her beliefs about herself, her beliefs about others, and her commitment to learning more about herself. Questions she needs to answer are:

are my strengths? Weaknesses?
do I need from others?
iat do I have to offer other people?
/hat do I believe is right for others?

Answering such questions is often difficult and may be painful. However, an effective counsellor should continually strive to know herself. Counsellors must be committed to continuous personal growth both in training and real life situations, and must have the courage and confidence to undertake the in-depth personal analysis they ask of clients. It must be stressed that personal development is an on-going process, and that as a person changes, the questions above will require new answers. It will be necessary for the counsellor periodically to answer the questions, 'Should I be a counsellor? Why?' and also to recognise that her readiness or suitability to counsel will vary as her own circumstances change. There will be times when she will have to sort out her own difficulties before she can resume counselling others. The important thing to recognise is that increased awareness of herself and her motives will enable her to work more effectively with others.

EXERCISE 2.1

1 Discuss with four or five others your reasons for wanting to become a counsellor. Afterwards, evaluate your participation. How open, searching, and honest were you in your statements about yourself? Did you hold back some reasons and instead say what you felt was safe and acceptable? How did others feel about your degree of openness?
2 In pairs, complete the following sentences:
   As a counsellor or helper –
   (a) I am becoming the kind of person who . . .
   (b) My strengths are . . .
   (c) My weaknesses are . . .
   (d) What I need most from people is . . .
   (e) What I give to people most of the time is . . .
   When both people have completed these statements, discuss the following questions in the larger group:
   (a) How open, searching, and honest were you in your statements about yourself?
   (b) Which statements were the easiest to complete? Most difficult? Why?

(c) What did you learn about yourself?
3 Using the information and self-knowledge gain
exercises above, write a one-page statement of y
motivations to be a counsellor. The last sentence sh
assessment of how honest and open you believe your
to be. Keep this statement and refer to it frequently as   progress through this book or your training course. Alter and amend
your statement at any time you wish. Do not share your statement with others unless you want to do so.

THE COUNSELLOR'S PERSONAL CULTURAL HISTORY

A major area of the counsellor's self-knowledge is her personal
cultural history and its influences on her present views of people
and society. Such awareness should include a review of how a
counsellor's family of origin has affected the ways she thinks and
feels about herself – her values and beliefs about religion,
morality, politics, race and gender issues, etc. It is helpful to focus
on specific topics from one's family of origin, such as who
constituted the family and what kinds of relationships existed
among them, what rules operated and what sanctions and rewards
supported them, how decisions were typically made and how the
family dealt with tensions and crises. Discussing family photographs can be a valuable aid to recall and discussion of how one's
family actually operated and how it might still influence one's
behaviour as an adult. It can also be helpful to discuss one's
family history further back, by considering one's grandparents and
great-grandparents and the ways in which their life experiences
may still be relevant to one's own.

Exercise 2.2

1 Your family of origin:
   (a) Choose 3–4 early family photos (when you were about 3
       to 12 years old) to share with two or three other people.
       When describing your family as they appear in the photos,
       try to identify the roles various family members played, the
       rules for interacting that operated, and the groupings of child-
       ren and/or adults and children that had a significant influ-
       ence on the family's functioning. Try to gain a clearer
       understanding of how your family of origin has affected
       your present values and beliefs.
   (b) Draw a floor plan of the house in which you spent a
       significant amount of time as a child. Describe the floor plan
       to the others in your small group. As you do, look for

significant factors that identify your family's functioning. For example, how were bedrooms allocated? Who was placed where? Which areas of the house were private? Public? What activities could be done where, and why? Again, try to gain a clearer understanding of how your family of origin affected your present values and beliefs.

2 Your cultural background:
   (a) Choose some object that represents some important aspect(s) of your cultural heritage. Discuss your object with others in your group and describe what cultural values, ideas, or beliefs it embodies and how those cultural values have influenced you as a person and as a counsellor.
   (b) Choose one of your favourite childhood stories or poems. Read it again looking for the cultural values and beliefs that it embodies. Discuss with others in your group how those values have influenced you as a person and as a counsellor.

DEVELOPING SELF-AWARENESS

A preliminary step in developing overall self-awareness involves counsellors experiencing and enjoying their inner and external worlds through the senses. In the following exercises, try to be open to new sensations and feelings without controlling or analysing them. Be relaxed and receptive to whatever happens.

EXERCISE 2.3

To experience awareness through the various senses:

1 Close your eyes and sit quietly in a comfortable position. As you begin to relax become aware of all the sounds around you. Gradually become aware of sounds within you. Discuss your experience with others.
2 Again sitting quietly with your eyes closed, reach out and explore your surroundings through touching. Notice textures, shapes, temperatures. As a variation, have someone hand you a series of objects to touch (eg, pencil, apple, cloth, metal, plastic). Discuss your experience with others.
3 Sit looking at an object (eg, book, cup, handbag, shoe). Be aware of all the details of that object: colour, shape, texture. Next look at another person. Do not become involved in a staring contest; merely see what the other person really looks like. Discuss your experience with others.

4 Sitting with your eyes closed have someone pass various scents under your nose (eg, flower, cheese, orange, chocolate, ink). Visualise all of the images that come to mind. Discuss your experience with others.

5 Sitting with your eyes closed have someone place various foods in your mouth. Taste them fully, using your tongue, lips, and teeth to experience the food. Discuss your experience with others.

The following diagram, known as the Johari Window (named after the originators, Joe Luft and Harry Ingham), presents a model for learning more about oneself. [*J. Luft*, Of Human Interaction, *Palo Alto, C.A: Mayfield Publishing, 1969*]

FIGURE 2.1 THE JOHARI WINDOW

	Known to Self	Unknown to Self
KNOWN TO OTHERS	**Free and Open:** You know and others know.	**Blind Self:** You don't know but others do.
UNKNOWN TO OTHERS	**Hidden Self:** You know but others do not.	**Unknown Self:** You don't know and others don't know.

Since becoming a counsellor involves increasing self-awareness, the goal should be to make the 'Free and Open' portion larger and the other three areas correspondingly smaller. The process of becoming self-aware and increasing self-understanding involves two important behaviours. First, counsellors must take risks by revealing parts of themselves to others. Secondly, a counsellor must be willing to ask for and receive feedback from others, about how she affects them and how well her behaviour matches her intentions.

Risk-taking involves trying out new behaviours, sharing thoughts and feelings with others and attempting to do those things which might be difficult. In these ways a counsellor begins to discover more about her abilities and limitations, and how people perceive her and react to her.

EXERCISE 2.4

In groups of two or three share information about yourself (ie, self-disclose) by orally completing the following statements:

1 Joining a new group makes me feel . . .
2 I like people to think I am . . .
3 When things are getting me down, I . . .
4 At this moment I feel . . .
5 When I first met you, I thought . . .
6 This exercise . . .

When all of the questions have been completed, discuss what you have just done by answering the following:

1 How did you feel while doing this exercise?
2 Which questions were easiest to answer? Most difficult?
3 Did you use objective and factual information about yourself to answer the questions, or subjective and feeling information? Which is more revealing of yourself? Why?
4 What did you learn about yourself?

This exercise can be made more or less intense or threatening by each person pairing up with, for example, someone they like, dislike, trust, distrust, etc.

EXERCISE 2.5

To risk doing something new or difficult, think of a situation or activity that you have wanted to change, challenge, confront, or attempt, but have never been able to before. For example, you may want to meet a certain stranger, sort out a misunderstanding with a workmate, or volunteer to lead an activity. Think of ways you could accomplish your goal. Choose the one you think is the best and put it into action. Later, discuss the results with others. Why did it succeed? Fail? How do you feel having done it? Was it worth the risk?

Feedback from others provides a counsellor with a valuable source of information. A counsellor must be prepared to learn from more than her own experience so that she can change, modify, and be aware of which of her behaviours are appropriate and which are not.

In giving and receiving feedback counsellors will be most effective if they observe the following guidelines:

1 Give feedback when it is requested. Ask for it only when it is desired.
2 Focus on specific behaviours and avoid sweeping, judgemental statements about a person's character or personality.
3 Use simple, non-technical language when describing another's behaviour.
4 Give feedback on behaviour the other person can control and change.
5 Give feedback as soon after the event or behaviour as possible. Do not store it up for later use.
6 Feedback should be positive as well as negative. People need to know their strengths as well as their weaknesses.
7 Accept the feedback as given, without misconstruing or generalising the specific content.
8 The receiver should have an opportunity to react to the feedback and check its accuracy with others.

EXERCISE 2.6

Seeing yourself as others see you is a powerful method of learning about yourself. There are a number of structured situations that can be used to encourage constructive feedback and sharing of perceptions.

1 Pair up with someone you have had some contact with already. Complete the following:
(a) You seem like the kind of person who . . .
(b) If you were angry, I would expect you to be . . .
(c) If you were happy, I would expect you to be . . .
(d) I appreciate you most when you . . .
(e) What I like about you right now is . . .
2 Reverse roles with your partner. Speak as though you were your partner. Try to describe yourself as you think your partner sees you. When finished, discuss what happened.

THE COUNSELLOR'S PERSONAL QUALITIES

Although there is no clear pattern of personal qualities or characteristics that the effective counsellor must possess, the following are desirable: flexibility, warmth, acceptance of others, open-mindedness, empathy, self-awareness, genuineness, respect for others, non-dominance, and objectivity. To state that they are essential is quite another matter. Researching these qualities is complicated by a number of factors such as imprecision of language, problems of control and measurement, and usefulness of the results in other situations. In trying to describe the effective counsellor the best that can be done seems to be to supplement research findings with expert opinion, personal experience, and common sense.

Perhaps a more useful way of indicating the personal qualities desirable in the counsellor would be to describe three areas of counselling in which they are important: the counsellor as a model, the counselling relationship, and the counsellor's courage to counsel.

The counsellor as a model. Modelling takes place in most learning situations. Essentially it is a means of learning through imitating the actions of others. In counselling, clients imitate the counsellor's actions and take certain of her beliefs and attitudes as their own. This process is inevitable and beyond the counsellor's control. A counsellor, however, should be aware of and accepting of herself, her values and behaviours, so that she presents a consistent model for effective relating and problem-solving. Such characteristics as being open, non-biased, non-judgemental, sensitive and caring can then be seen as directly related to effective helping.

The counselling relationship. It is widely accepted by practitioners and theorists that the relationship between counsellor and client is an important aspect of counselling. Effective counsellors are those who can establish caring, non-threatening relationships with their clients in which both feel safe and secure enough to interact as real, spontaneous people. The quality of this relationship can itself be therapeutic and depends very largely on the counsellor being a real person.

The courage to counsel. In order to help others, counsellors need courage and self-confidence. There are many times when it would be easier for a counsellor to opt out of helping: to ignore a plea for help; make excuses for not wanting to become involved with another person; or judge a situation to be hopeless, unrealistic, trivial, or outside her area of competence. To make a commitment to help another person carries with it responsibilities and uncertainties. Anyone who seriously intends to become an effective counsellor must be willing to accept those responsibilities and uncertainties and place herself in situations of personal, emotional, interpersonal, and vocational risk. Again, the counsellor must be prepared to function as a whole and real person rather than as a performer acting only within safely prescribed limits.

ROLE-PLAYING AS A COUNSELLING SKILL

Much of living and learning involves the playing of roles. This is particularly true in counselling, both in training to be a counsellor and working therapeutically with clients. Role-playing itself is not a unique or unusual form of behaviour. All relationships involve role-playing, since people relate to others as holders of a certain role, status, or position.

Role-playing is the process of acting the part of a real or imagined person. When used in counsellor training, it has a number of potential benefits for counsellors:

1 By role-playing real situations early in training, counsellors can feel free to make mistakes and try new behaviours without worrying about adverse effects on clients.
2 Role-playing enables counsellors to experience what it feels like to be a client and to develop ability and confidence in portraying and expressing feelings and ideas.
3 Role-playing helps counsellors to learn by doing rather than by merely discussing techniques and strategies in an abstract and intellectual manner.
4 Role-playing is useful in learning about the dynamics of forming and building a relationship.

There are difficulties in role-playing as a training device, however. Many people find it threatening. This threat should be faced and overcome by intending counsellors. Also, some people are so guarded or unimaginative in expressing their feelings that they are ineffective in role-playing, or they portray clients who are difficult to work with, emotionally dull, and unresponsive. Those who have this difficulty should practise expressing their own feelings, even exaggerating them, until they are able to express easily and realistically a wide range of emotions. A related problem is that of trying to beat or frustrate the counsellor by playing an impossibly difficult client. The aim of role-playing is not to compete against a counsellor but to simulate a real counselling situation.

Role-playing may be criticised as being artificial. While there is some justification for this view, most role-players report that they very quickly forget about themselves and become totally engrossed in the part they are playing. If individuals persist in labelling the situation as artificial and refuse to take part, they may be avoiding something in themselves and should be asked to evaluate their stance. Role-playing, whether from detailed, scripted material or from wholly imagined material, is ultimately an expression of each player's self, her beliefs, attitudes, and feelings. Players become engrossed in their parts because the roles they are playing are really extensions of themselves. Thus, whatever the supposed difficulties of role-playing as a training device, it allows people an opportunity to experience new situations, practise new behaviours, reveal themselves in safety and gain confidence and skill in relating to others.

In counselling, much of what a counsellor asks, encourages, or suggests a client do, involves acting differently or changing aspects of his behaviour; in short, playing new or more effective roles. The counsellor should be willing and able to model the behaviours she wants the client to try.

EXERCISE 2.7

1 Group role-playing. Someone from the group plays the role of client while the rest of the group simultaneously play counsellor. The client can role-play any problem, concern or situation he wishes. As the counsellors begin to respond, the client should deal with one response at a time, saying, 'Yes, that would encourage me to continue because . . .', or 'No, that would not encourage me to continue because . . . '. When a 'Yes' response is received from the client, the group should continue as though in a real counselling situation.

When finished, the client describes what it felt like to be a client, and the exercise is repeated with another person playing the part of client. This method of role-playing minimises the threat to any one person by having several people play counsellor at once. It also gives those playing counsellor some information about how effective their responses are, and at the same time forces the client to be aware of how he feels in that role and in response to what is said to him.

2 The large group divides into smaller groups of three or four. Two people role-play an interview situation as in the first exercise above. Those people not role-playing should act as observers and comment on how authentic the role-play seems and how helpful or otherwise the counsellor's statements seem. Repeat this situation until all the people have played counsellor and client.

3 Finally, people pair up and discuss real situations with their partners. Everyone has something they are concerned about and which they can safely share with another person. The topic does not have to be a major concern or worry, but should be current. The counsellor's aim is to listen, understand, and respond as helpfully as she can. After 15 minutes, switch roles and repeat. This variation makes the situation more authentic and gives the person playing client the opportunity to experience what it is like to ask for and receive help.

3

Beginning the problem-solving process

Here we examine the counselling skills involved in the first stage of the problem-solving process – problem definition. The Introduction looks at a complete list of skills, arranged in the sequence of problem-solving stages that were set out in the first chapter.

INTRODUCTION

It is unlikely that every skill listed will be used with every client, but counsellors should aim to become proficient in all of the skills so that they have a wide repertoire on which to draw. Though we have arranged them in a sequence, there is no finality about the placement of any particular skill, but in general the earlier ones can always be used throughout the process, while the later ones depend for their effectiveness on the client's problems and goals having been clearly defined. Once the counsellor has acquired the skills, it is most important that he have in mind as clearly as possible where he and his client are in the process of solving the client's problem. It is unfortunately true that some counsellors miss out important steps, for example, trying to move to a solution before the problem has been clearly defined. Another mistake is to seize on the first solution likely to solve the problem, without first considering alternative possibilities.

These steps in problem-solving are so important that if any are missed out or not covered adequately, the counsellor will probably have to backtrack in order to help the client reach a satisfactory solution. While it is best to be as systematic as possible and not have to go back, counselling seldom proceeds in strict linear fashion. Thus to have to return to an earlier stage and to some of the earlier skills does not necessarily mean that the counsellor has been ineffective. The important thing is to deal with all the stages in the process adequately.

It should also be noted that effective counselling can sometimes be condensed into quite a short time. If there is a good working relationship and a high state of readiness on the part of the client, all the main steps of problem-solving may be covered satisfactorily in less than forty minutes. With complex issues and resistant or less motivated clients, however, it may take several lengthy sessions before the problem is clearly defined.

Problem definition

It is important that clients' concerns be stated in problem form, and the counsellor's first task is often to help his client to do this as precisely as possible. This does not mean that the counsellor should keep quizzing the client, because people often seek help because they do not know exactly what the problem is, or because they find it difficult or embarrassing to discuss it with others. It is frequently necessary, however, to help clients make more specific their vague general concerns. Posing the following sorts of questions and getting full answers to them could be useful at this stage: 'What do you see as the problem? Can you give me an example? How often does this sort of thing happen?'

Skills at this stage include:

Getting started	**Thinking aloud**
Open invitation to talk	**Immediacy**
Sorting issues	**Using silence**
Open and closed questions	**Identifying feelings**
Topic following	**Expressing feelings**
Minimal encouragers	**Reflection**
Active listening	**Accurate understanding**
Engaging reluctant clients	

Goal setting

After the problem has been defined it becomes the basis for setting goals to solve it. The way in which a goal is stated makes a great deal of difference to the effectiveness of counselling. If a goal is stated in vague general terms, it will usually be impossible to know how to reach it. Counsellors should therefore help clients to say what they want to achieve in terms that are as precise as possible. Getting answers to the following kinds of questions should help clients to express their goals so that steps towards

31

them can be worked out: 'What would you like to do that you cannot do now? What would you like to do better? What changes would you like others to make?'

Skills at this stage include:

Direct questioning	Giving advice
Dealing with discrepancies	Influencing
Setting goals	Giving directions
Supporting and encouraging	Using personal
Interpretation	examples
Giving information	Advising a delay
	Gaining commitment

Strategy selection

Once the client has selected one or more goals to aim at and they have been expressed in terms that are as specific as possible, the next step in the process is to work out how to achieve those goals. For some clients the task at this point is really one of choice: they may already have the resources needed to achieve the goal, but are finding it difficult to establish priorities or to choose between alternatives that seem equally attractive but may be incompatible. For those clients who already know what it is they want to achieve, the task is one of change, ie, how to alter their present environment, or their own behaviour, or that of other people.

Skills at this stage include:

Anticipating situations
Providing models
Role-playing
Using rewards

Implementation of strategy

The counsellor's task at this stage is to help the client to work out in detail how to put into practice whatever strategy was decided at the previous stage. Those whose problem was essentially one of choice may need help in following up on the implications of their decision. Where change was needed, the counsellor's tasks would include planning, teaching, and support.

Skills at this stage include:

Making records
Bodily awareness and relaxation
Thoughts and imagery
Desensitisation
Mixing strategies
Homework

Evaluation

If goals have been precisely stated and suitable strategies selected and implemented, the important task of evaluation will be relatively simple. It will be a matter of checking what has been achieved against what was hoped for. Counsellor and client should decide in advance how the evaluation will be made – by regular checks on progress towards the goals, or by a delayed check on the outcome as a whole. If the outcome is not satisfactory, it may be necessary to go back through part of the problem-solving process again, perhaps to choose a different goal or a different strategy.

Skills at this stage include:

Assessing results
Summarising
Generalising
Referral
Termination

THE SKILLS OF PROBLEM DEFINITION

Getting started

The first contact between a counsellor and a client usually has significant effects on what happens. A relationship of trust needs to be built up and sustained if change is eventually to take place. A client usually responds to signs of sensitivity, respect, and empathy from her counsellor. She will want to feel that her counsellor has the ability to see a situation as she does, to feel with her and to assume her frame of reference. She will usually respond to a friendly, caring, and considerate manner and to being helped to be specific about her feelings and experiences. Sensitivity, respect, empathy, and concreteness are among the most important factors in facilitating a counselling relationship.

The client may wonder whether she is free to express her real concerns. In effect she sums up the counsellor and the counselling situation while responding. She may consider a series of internal questions such as: Am I welcome? Can I trust this counsellor? Is a relationship possible? Will it be satisfying? Can this counsellor help me?

Answers to such questions will be provided not merely by words. Other, often more subtle and powerful means of communication are the physical setting, the way the client is greeted, the counsellor's gestures and tone of voice, and the presence or absence of distractions. All of these convey messages to the client.

From the outset it is vital that the counsellor be alert to the many factors that influence progress. These include being a good objective observer of the client and of the whole physical and social setting, helping the client to express herself in her own way, and being aware of his own role as a possible stimulus to the client and a model for her to copy.

This chapter will examine all the skills listed under problem definition. Because counselling occurs in a reciprocal relationship, the counsellor's awareness of himself will also be considered. This counselling relationship is a dynamic one involving specific behaviours that can be identified and practised.

IS THE CLIENT VOLUNTARY OR INVOLUNTARY?

This question considers whether the client has freely chosen to come, whether she has been persuaded, or whether the counsellor has asked to see her, as may often happen in a school setting.

After the initial greetings it is often helpful to deal with this issue straight away. A voluntary client may be easier to work with initially because a decision has already been made to seek help. This implies at least some recognition of a problem and some desire to change. Sometimes, however, it may mask a desire to use the counsellor in a manipulative way.

In some settings some clients perceive the counsellor as someone who can be used to ease pressures that are legitimately exerted by other people. As soon as the counsellor senses that this may be occurring, he should test this hunch, if necessary by discussing it directly with the client. Coyness, guile, and game-playing on the part of the client should not be paid back in kind. The counsellor's model of open and direct expression of feelings and perceptions is the best counter to clients' attempts to 'con' him.

Another example of an attempt at manipulation is the attempt to put the counsellor down. This may take the form of questioning or scoffing at his experience, methods, and qualifications. If the client should object on a point that is valid and relevant to the discussion, the counsellor should simply acknowledge this and then move back to the discussion as smoothly as possible. Counsellors who feel defensive about such matters and attempt to debate or deny the point or to justify themselves, will usually make an awkward situation worse. It is probably best to say calmly, 'I don't think that's relevant here.'

With an involuntary client our experience suggests that it can be very productive to deal immediately with the client's reactions to being present.
The counsellor may:

1 State who referred the client.
2 Give the reason for the referral, eg, 'Mr James is concerned because you have been very quiet in class lately and the standard of your work has slipped.'
3 Tell the client what might be offered by a counsellor.
4 Invite the client to express feelings about being in this situation. Is she angry? afraid? puzzled? uncertain?
5 Emphasise that the client is free to remain or leave. Often, acceptance of the freedom to leave without being pursued is the first step in establishing the trust which will lead to the client's voluntary return.
6 Suggest that while the client may reject you as her helper there are other sources of help for her problem. Name these sources if the client is interested.

In some instances clients may continue to be reluctant or reticent about participating in counselling. Techniques for engaging these clients are discussed more fully on page 51.

WHAT BACKGROUND INFORMATION IS AVAILABLE AND HOW MUCH IS NEEDED?

The answers to this question will be determined by the counselling setting, the nature and extent of the problem, the purpose of the counselling, the relevance of background information, the preferences of the counsellor, and the availability of the information.
The setting. Detailed information may be more pertinent in the clinical setting of a psychiatric unit where long-term, in-depth counselling is to take place than in, for example, a Citizen's Advice Bureau where the contact may be limited to one visit.
The nature and extent of the problem. Comprehensive, detailed background information may be desirable if major personality change is sought but is unnecessary if the problem is one of learning certain skills such as how to be more assertive or how to conduct oneself during a job interview.
Purpose of counselling. If a person wishes to free herself from patterns of emotional reaction and behaviour that have their roots

in her upbringing it can be pertinent to know something of the family dynamics. However, if the client seeks information on job requirements, legal rights, or child development, background information on the client may not be essential or even relevant.

Relevance. Information about educational qualifications would be relevant in vocational counselling but probably not in marriage guidance. A social worker engaged in a welfare inquiry would be vitally interested in details of family income but this would be irrelevant to a school counsellor dealing with a conflict between peers.

THE COUNSELLOR'S PREFERENCES

1 A counsellor may prefer to gain his impressions of the client and his analysis of the problem from first-hand contact rather than be influenced by background information. He may want to leave his mind free from preconceptions or from the interpretations of other people.

2 A counsellor may prefer to obtain background information incidentally during the course of an interview.

3 A counsellor may prefer to obtain background information before first meeting the client, in the interests of greater understanding of the client, economy of time or as a guide to leading in the interview.

4 A counsellor may prefer to obtain information in a structured interview as a way of beginning a relationship.

AVAILABILITY OF INFORMATION

In some settings, such as schools and medical centres, comprehensive records are available to be consulted by workers within that setting. The information may also be available to social workers, psychologists and others with a professional interest in the client. In other settings and circumstances information may not be divulged in order to preserve confidentiality. Sometimes information may be offered directly by the client, or she may give permission for it to be obtained elsewhere. The credibility of the source of background information is an aspect to be considered.

TYPES OF INFORMATION

It is unlikely that a voluntary rather than a professional counsellor would need information on all the following topics but these are the areas generally included in a comprehensive case history or case study.

Name	**Address**	**Race**
Dates of Contacts	**Date of Birth**	**Place of Birth**

Problem. (Nature, onset, seriousness, duration, previous attempts to deal with it. Opinions and attitudes of others, eg, parents, teachers, employers, medical personnel.)

Family. (Names, ages, occupations and sex of family members, socio-economic status, cultural patterns, family relationships, health problems, religion.)

Physical Health. (Hearing, eyesight, serious illnesses, current health, appearance.)

Psychological Test Results.

Educational History and Achievements.

Social Development. (Sociability and adaptability, friends, participation in groups.)

Emotional Development. (General mental health, stability, self-image, predominant moods, signs of stress, eg, tics, twitching, tears, stuttering, tantrums.)

Work Experience. (Place and dates of employment. Type of work performed. Attitude towards work. Vocational plans and aspirations.)

General Summing-Up.

THE FIRST SIGHTING AND MEETING

The client and counsellor immediately begin sizing up each other. Each begins a process of observing and silently questioning. An internal dialogue such as that in column 2 of Figure 3.1 (page 39) may take place in the counsellor's mind.

The counsellor should be aware of the following:

1 *Client's physical appearance*
   Would it create problems for the client?
   Does it give a clue about health? about self-image? (eg, the tidiness of clothing, personal hygiene.)

2 *Manner and bearing*
   Does the client appear nervous? withdrawn? aggressive? defensive? passive?

3 *Movement and gestures*
   Is the client still or moving about?
   What is she doing with her hands? her head? her feet?
   What is the possible meaning of her movements and gestures?

4 *Posture and stance*
   Is the client upright? hunched over? standing freely? supporting herself on furniture? What does this mean?

5 *Surroundings*
Is the counselling setting private? relatively informal?
Is the decor of the room warm and relaxing?
Is there freedom from extraneous noise?
Are the seats comfortable? well-placed?
Is the counsellor behind a desk? beside it? in front of it?

6 *Differences in social status*
Does the client's clothing indicate poverty? wealth? social position? state of mind?

7 *Physical distance*
Is the client so close to you as to be threatened by the closeness?
Are the counsellor and client comfortably apart?

8 *Eye contact*
Is the client able to look you in the eye or does she avoid your gaze?

SELF-AWARENESS

Counselling occurs in a reciprocal relationship. The client, as well as the counsellor, is observing and reacting (see column 3 of Figure 3.1, page 39). Success in counselling depends considerably upon the client's perceptions of the counsellor's manner and behaviour. The client will be aware of and react to the counsellor's eye contact, posture, gesture, and manner. She will react to the length and delay of the counsellor's responses, interruptions, amount of talk, and voice quality.

Good eye contact involves looking at the client when she is talking and using glances that express interest and acceptance. A piercing stare, look of blankness, or avoidance of the client's gaze will be disconcerting to her. People tend to use eye contact more when listening than when speaking.

The counsellor should sit facing the client in an open, relaxed manner, and far enough away from her to feel comfortable. His hands should be kept relatively still and his facial expressions friendly. Slouching, playing with a pen, frowning or too much movement are distracting.

Getting the client to talk freely is important in the initial stages. A warm, pleasant tone of voice, simple language and medium volume make the counsellor's conversation more effective. A counsellor who talks too much discourages the client who may well feel that her ideas are not important. If the counsellor can delay responses naturally, there is an increased chance that the client will talk and explain more. Short counsellor responses also

FIGURE 3.1 A POSSIBLE INTERNAL DIALOGUE ON FIRST MEETING

ATTRIBUTE	COUNSELLOR OBSERVATIONS AND QUESTIONS	CLIENT OBSERVATIONS AND QUESTIONS
Physical Appearance	She is very thin and pale . . . Is she ill? under strain? depressed? Her hair is untidy and her blouse has a button missing . . . Is she depressed?	He's so big and tall . . . reminds me of my father. It's frightening. Can I trust him?
Manner	She is withdrawn. Is she depressed? reluctant to be here?	His voice is warm and friendly. He looks me in the eye and smiles.
Bearing	She is hunched over, holding herself tightly. Is she afraid of me? of the situation? of revealing her anxiety?	He looks relaxed and calm. He is upright but not stiff. His hands are at his side. He seems at ease. Can I relax too?
Movement and Gestures	She is turning her head away from me, twisting her hands, moving her left foot up and down. She twitches. Is she very tense and anxious?	He is fairly still but not stiff and tense.
Posture	She is sitting hunched up on the edge of the chair. Is she very tense? defensive?	He is leaning slightly towards me. His hands are loosely clasped.
Stance	She is turned away from me, presenting her shoulder, not her face.	He is seated to the side of me, facing me. I don't feel as if I am being confronted.
Surroundings	I've told the secretary not to put any phone calls through for half an hour. Hope she remembers. It's a bit cold . . . Should I turn on the heater?	It's private in here. I like the gold curtains. This chair is comfortable. Can I relax now? Maybe?
Eye Contact	She can't look me in the eye consistently. She darts quick glances at me now and then.	His eyes look warm. I want to look at him but I can't manage to keep looking at him yet. I think I can trust him.

encourage this, as does a minimum of interruption. The client can feel that she is accepted, worthwhile, and free to speak.

The following exercises are designed to allow the participants to experience the effects of various physical surroundings, gestures, eye contact, and other attributes, as discussed above. (Leaders may find it valuable to have course members do the exercises before reading those sections.) The exercises may be done as demonstrations before a large group or they may be done in small groups with one participant taking the part of the counsellor, another the client, and the others acting as observers.

EXERCISE 3.1*

Client Reactions
After each exercise the client should share her reactions to what happened. She may share with the whole group or with her small group only.
1 Physical Conditions
   (a) Experiment with three chair positions.

   In which situation did the client feel most comfortable?
   (b) Vary the counsellor's position in relation to a desk.

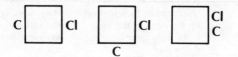

   In what way did the client feel differently towards the counsellor's being in each of these positions in relation to the desk?
2 Eye Contact
   (a) Counsellor looks at ceiling, out the window, at the bookshelf, anywhere but directly at the client.
   (b) Counsellor makes eye contact with the client without staring her down.

*Throughout this book, exercises that are marked with an asterisk have the answers provided in Answers to Exercises, p 155–158.

3 Movement, Gesture, Posture, Stance
   (a) Counsellor sits upright at his desk, plays with a pencil, bends a paperclip, taps his foot against the desk.
   (b) Counsellor leans against the wall and waves his arms around while talking.
   (c) Counsellor leans forward towards the client while already sitting close with his knees almost touching hers.
   (d) Counsellor sits on his chair in a relaxed way, hands held loosely, and leans forward slightly.
4 Greeting
   (a) Counsellor with his tie askew and hair ruffled is looking in the filing cabinet. Greets client with 'Just a minute will you.' Continues to search the files, takes out a folder, slams the drawer shut, produces a comb, combs his hair, straightens his tie and at last says 'What did you say your name was again?'
   (b) Replay in a more welcoming manner.

EXERCISE 3.2*

[*Adapted from D.W. Johnson*, Reaching out, *Englewood Cliffs, N.J. Prentice Hall, 1972.*]

Counsellor Reactions
Ask a counsellor what the client might be experiencing.

1 Client sits perched on the edge of the chair, twisting her hands and staring at the floor.
2 Client sits upright, holding herself tightly, hands clasped firmly and launches into a complaint in self-righteous tones.
3 Client sits down and bursts into tears.
4 Client refuses to speak.

EXERCISE 3.3

Self-awareness
1 Eye Contact
   (a) Form pairs. Stand 1–2 metres away from your partner. One partner at a time looks at the eyes of the other and then says what the other is looking at.
   (b) Each in turn looks at his partner's forehead, nose, chin, neck, and shoulders in that sequence. See when your partner can tell you are *not* looking into his eyes.
   (c) Maintain eye contact with your partner while paying him a compliment and receiving his response. Repeat while crit-

icism is offered. (If you do not know your partner you may have to confine your compliment or criticism to outward appearance or clothing.)

2 Voice Quality

(a) Form pairs. Make the statement, 'Hullo, Paul. I'm pleased you could come', in two ways:
    (i) In a flat, uninterested way.
    (ii) In a warm, welcoming way.
    Listen carefully to the difference and invite your partner to react.

(b) Carry on your conversation from the above opening statement. Get your partner to comment on the quality of your voice.

3 Counsellor Responses

(a) A training course leader should make a tape of a segment of conversation demonstrating effective and ineffective use of timing and length of responses and interruptions. Group members should be invited to comment.

(b) Alternatively, such a segment of conversation could be role-played to the group.

Open invitation to talk

If the client is invited to talk freely, instead of being subjected to a series of questions, she is more likely to present her problem. In part the invitation to speak will be conveyed by the counsellor's posture, manner, gesture, and tone of voice. The words used will make the message explicit.

After the client has been received into the room, greeted and seated, a statement can be made or a question asked that tells her she is welcome and recognised, and that it is her right to define the problem. It also says that the counsellor is ready to listen and help.

For example:

'How can I help you?'
'Tell me what is bothering you.'
'My secretary said that when you phoned you were concerned about . . .'
'What's on your mind?'

The counsellor should use a warm, accepting tone and words that are natural to him. He should avoid stereotyping beginning statements or using false humour. He should also be wary of imputing 'worry' or 'problems' unless the client has already used such terms. Occasionally counsellors are faced with clients who are initially resistant or reluctant to participate in counselling. Techniques for engaging these clients are discussed on page 51.

EXERCISE 3.4*

In pairs, alternating the role of counsellor and client, give open invitations to speak to the following:
(a) A distraught mother whose teenage son is disrupting family life.
(b) A middle-aged man just made redundant.
(c) A teenage girl with a career inquiry.
  Discuss the effectiveness of your statements.

Sorting issues
Some clients may respond to the counsellor's open invitation to talk with a torrent of problems or concerns. They may talk non-stop for several minutes and describe a number of related or unrelated problems. Since it is necessary for both the client and counsellor to fully understand and clarify the client's concerns, the counsellor can begin by responding in a way that will help the client sort the issues. This is done by simply listing the concerns the client has mentioned and inviting her to select the one that she thinks should be dealt with first. For example:
Client: I've had it with school! The work is too hard; the English teacher picks on me; Mum and Dad nag me about not having enough homework to do; and two of my best friends have been ignoring me lately.
Counsellor: You have mentioned several things: the difficulty of the work; the English teacher's attitude toward you; your parents' concerns about your lack of homework; and problems with two of your friends. Which of these do you want to talk about first?
The skill of sorting issues indicates that the counsellor has been listening, is actively concerned, and is willing to focus on issues the client thinks are most pressing. Also, by encouraging the client to think more clearly about her problems and to list them in the order she wishes to deal with them, the beginning of an effective model of problem-solving is presented to the client. To aid this process, either the counsellor or the client can make a list of the problems as they are described. This will underscore the importance of being clear and will help to guide and form the counselling interaction in successive sessions.

EXERCISE 3.5

In pairs, alternating the role of counsellor and client, use the skill of sorting issues in response to the following:

1 'Nothing is going right. I hate work, can't stand the sight of the place. And when I get home, the kids jump on me with a whole day's demands and problems. I never get any help from anyone – always have to do everything myself.'

2 'Well, let's see. I guess it's really my own lack of self-confidence. I mean, I suppose I should know how to do those things, but I don't. Where would I even go to learn? And my parents don't really help things. They just criticise me for being lazy. What can I say to them? What do I do?'

3 'I'm trying to decide what subjects to take next year. I would really like to do more art, but Dad says that I need all the science I can get. Since I won't be going to university, is there any use in taking physics and chemistry? I don't really like them and can't see me ever using any of it. And that's another problem. What work will I be able to do if I don't pass my exams?'

Open and closed questions

Open-ended questions or statements invite the client to continue talking by suggesting that she give more details about a topic she has introduced.

For example:

'What is it about your mother that frustrates you so much?'

Open questions are best used when explanations, opinions, and examples are needed. They are particularly important in the early stages of an interview when the counsellor needs to know as much about the client's concern as possible. Beginning questions with: what? when? how? where? why? is one useful way of making them open.

By contrast, closed questions are best used when factual information or a 'yes' or 'no' response is all that is required. Closed questions tend to shut off a conversation and covertly suggest that the client should be quiet and answer only what is asked of her. A series of such questions or statements can sound like an interrogation.

For example:

'It sounds as if your mother frustrates you.'
'Yes.'

'Does she make you angry too?'
'Yes.'
'You'd like to get away from her?'
'Not really.'
'Oh, I thought you'd want to leave home.'
'No.'

Before using an open or closed question, the counsellor should decide what kinds of information are needed. Answers to open questions will tend to give the counsellor fuller explanations, more complete information, and useful clues or free information to follow up and thus keep the interview going. Open questions also indicate to the client that she is free to lead the discussion where she wants. Answers to closed questions, on the other hand, will yield important factual information, or confirm or disconfirm a point or opinion. They can indicate that the counsellor is listening, is thinking about the client's problem and may be forming some hypothesis about the problem.

It is important to remember that open questions are not to be thought of as a 'good' counselling skill and closed questions as a 'bad' skill. Both can be effective when used appropriately.

EXERCISE 3.6*

1 Which of the following are open-ended?
   (a) Do you like peanuts?
   (b) Why did you return to school this year?
   (c) How would you get rid of such a nuisance?
   (d) Is it time to go home?
2 Rewrite the following as open-ended questions.
   (a) Did you enjoy the party?
   (b) Did you leave school because you wanted to earn money?
   (c) Have we got enough money to get home?
   (d) Did you get that jacket at a sale?

Topic following
Topic following is best thought of as an aim or focus, ie, as a means of attending to what it is that the client wants to discuss, and not as a discrete skill. In fact, any skill a counsellor chooses to use can indicate whether he has followed the topic or not. In essence, topic following means focusing on what the client has actually said rather than taking the topic in a new direction or adding to its meaning.

Topic following should be done consistently, especially in the early stages of counselling, before the counsellor has a clear and detailed picture of the client's concern. In a warm, attentive way the counsellor helps the client to go on exploring the topic to make her aware that he is really listening to her. In later stages of the relationship, it may become more appropriate for the counsellor to introduce new topics or check the accuracy of his own hypothesis about the client's predicament.

Examples of good topic following include the use of statements such as:

'I see what you mean.'
'Tell me more about it.'
'Would you explain that a bit more?'

EXERCISE 3.7*

Add a statement or question to each of the following client statements so that the topic is followed. You may write the statements, say them in pairs and, if desired, tape the dialogues.

1 'I can't seem to get a job. Whenever I go for an interview they say they'll get in touch but they never do.'
2 'My mother insists that I get home by 12 pm whenever I'm out. Sometimes that's just impossible.'
3 'I hate school! The teachers, the rules, the uniform, the lot!'

Minimal encouragers
Minimal encouragers are gestures, nods, single words or noises, body postures or repetitions of key words that indicate that the counsellor is interested and involved, but that the client is in control of deciding which way the interview will go. They should be used early in the contact within the natural flow of the dialogue. Examples include:

'Mmm'
'A-ha'
'Yes?'
'So?'
'Your mother?'

Minimal encouragers are effective in keeping the client talking, whereas too much talk from the counsellor may lose the client. She may easily get the message, 'This is not my interview. He wants to hear his own voice, not mine.'

EXERCISE 3.8

Practise using minimal encouragers in conversations you have at home, or at work or in counselling situations. Share any comments you may have about their use with others in your training course. Note the use of minimal encouragers while watching a TV programme.

Active listening

Listening is basic to all interviews. It requires that the counsellor be silent most of the time and use all his senses to get the total message. He listens with his ears to the words spoken and the tone of voice, with his mind to the underlying message, and with his eyes to the language of the body in its posture, bearing, and gestures. The counsellor also listens to himself: he notes his reactions to the message he is receiving and to the way he is coping with it. A number of specific listening skills will be covered in Chapter Four.

Active, accurate listening is vital throughout an interview but especially at the beginning when the counsellor usually takes a less verbally active part. The counsellor listens by tuning in with his being to the other person, concentrating on her, allowing her messages to be paramount. This is intended to communicate *empathy*, ie, to prove that the counsellor *heard, understood,* and *accepted* what has been said to him.

EXERCISE 3.9

1 Two group members have a conversation on an agreed topic where some personal feeling would be expressed. This takes 3 to 4 minutes.
2 One observer listens mainly to the client's words and summarises the message.
3 Another observer concentrates on the body language of the client.
4 The rest of the group can listen to the total message but also be especially aware of their own reactions to the client's statements.

The language of counselling

It is a sign of sensitivity to and respect for another person and her culture if a counsellor can understand and speak some of her language, formal and colloquial. This may include only greetings, salutations, common expressions, and important ideas, but even this basic knowledge can be evidence of a sincere effort to understand the client's culture. It is also imperative that counsellors use non-sexist language and avoid using terms that may be derogatory or demeaning to particular groups (eg, the aged, those with disabilities, etc.). Because language is so central to social interactions and can have such a powerful effect in defining reality for various groups, it may be important to alter its use in ways that will allow clients to change their perceptions of people and events. The following two sections describe ways in which both clients and counsellors can alter their use of language within the context of the counselling relationship.

A. THE CLIENT'S USE OF LANGUAGE

Counsellors need to pay close attention to their clients' use of language because it can indicate aspects of their functioning and their concerns that may not otherwise be readily apparent. For example, unusual emphases ('I'd *never* admit anything to *her*!'), striking omissions ('I'm scared.' – about what?), and elaborate rationalisations should prompt a counsellor to seek further explanations or consider possible meanings behind what a client has said. It may also be helpful to get a client to talk less when it appears that the client's verbosity helps her to avoid her anxieties and uncertainties. Sometimes, too, the counsellor can help a client to deal with issues more directly and positively by suggesting that the client use different language. Getting them to change some language patterns can be helpful, but counsellors should not over-prescribe how clients might speak. Additional ways in which counsellors may help clients include directing them to:

(a) use the active rather than the passive voice ('I did it.' rather than 'it just happened to me.');
(b) talk in the present tense rather than in the past or future tense ('I am doing it now.' rather than 'I'll work on that sometime.');
(c) express herself in personal rather than impersonal ways ('I feel awful.' rather than 'It leaves one feeling awful.');
(d) use statements instead of masking them as questions ('I don't want to do that.' rather than 'How could that help me?');
(e) rephrase current concerns so as to neither overstate nor minimise them ('It's hard to face her right now.' rather than 'I'll never be able to face her again.');

(f) identify feelings instead of denying or obscuring them with thoughts and explanations ('I'm angry!' rather than 'I think there are plenty of reasons why you should not have done that to me!');

(g) speak in concrete, specific terms rather than abstract, general terms ('I yelled at my younger sister today and she told my parents about it.' rather than 'I'm useless!');

(h) use the singular 'I' when speaking for herself and not the plural forms 'we' or 'us' ('I think the boss is being unfair.' rather than 'Everyone knows the boss is unfair.');

(i) use 'won't' instead of 'can't' to emphasise that the client is responsible for her decisions and has the power to change them ('I won't change.' rather than 'I can't change.');

(j) use 'want' instead of 'need' when that is what is really meant ('I want her to love me.' rather than 'I need her to love me.');

(k) drop frequently used qualifiers like 'maybe', 'may', 'possibly' when those are used to cushion critical statements or avoid taking a stance ('I *can* stand up to him!' rather than 'Well, maybe I can stand up to him.');

(l) repeat a particular statement, phrase, or word to highlight and clarify its real meaning ('You didn't do it; I let you.' Ask the client to repeat 'I *let* you!').

B. THE COUNSELLOR'S USE OF LANGUAGE

Besides listening to clients' language, counsellors should also become acutely aware of their own language patterns. The importance of this is often overlooked. There is enormous potential for counsellors to influence their clients' decision-making and actions through the latter adopting the counsellor's style. It is necessary, therefore, that counsellors become more careful in their use of language in counselling. Following are four aspects of a counsellor's language with illustrations of how they can be used to contribute to a more effective and open counselling relationship.

1 Establishing Rapport, Developing a Relationship.

Virtually every counselling theory emphasises the importance of establishing a trusting, working relationship with the client so that the process of counselling may proceed with the least hindrance. To accomplish this counsellors can try several things. They should engage in culturally appropriate small talk, to observe, even if briefly, the rituals of courtesy and socially appropriate greetings. The language used in this rapport building stage is usually simple and is merely the standard parlance of society. In addition, counsellors can attempt to join with or blend with a client's behaviour style or values by identifying a client's dominant features of language, values, or behaviour and then using some of those features in their own speech. In practice this could mean talking less or more, lightheartedly or seriously, rapidly or slowly, each depending on the client's style, or actually mimicking in a sympathetic way particular gestures, postures or movements.

2 Understanding the Counsellor's Preferred Language.
Every theory of counselling has its own technical language, its own jargon. Typically clients are either consciously taught this language or they unconsciously imitate their counsellor's dominant language features. It may well be more to the point ethically if, instead of imposing certain concepts and language forms on clients, counsellors were to increase their awareness of the dominant features of their own language. For example, the counsellor may notice that he repeatedly used feeling words, or diagnostic labels, or references to cognitive processes, or figures of speech, or polysyllabic words. While these language habits may not all be counterproductive in themselves, they could well impede the progress of counselling. Once aware of his own language style, including the jargon associated with his own theoretical orientation, the counsellor can more consciously attempt to match or alter the language style of his client.

3 The Intended Message versus the Actual Message.
Most of the time counsellors interact with their clients in purposeful, intentional ways. The interview has direction, and the counsellor's responses indicate that direction. However, it is often the case that the counsellor's intended message is not what is actually said. For example, the counsellor may use warm, supportive words but convey an underlying impatience or distance; or, the counsellor may change the topic of discussion merely to clarify an earlier client statement but in so doing convey an impression of being bored with the client. Furthermore, if the counsellor needs to know about something, he should ask. For example, if it is important to know how a client is getting along with her spouse, the counsellor should ask directly rather than hope that a vague, general inquiry like 'How are things at home?' will elicit the desired information.

When discrepancies occur between what was meant and what was actually said, the client may be left feeling unsure and confused. To overcome this, the counsellor can endeavour to say exactly what he means. Being more specific, more genuine, and more immediate (see the skills of Thinking Aloud and Immediacy) are ways of accomplishing this.

4 Statements or Questions as Autobiographical Material. The counsellor's use of language can tell a lot about himself as well as what he is trying to accomplish with his client. Thus, counsellors should strive to be more aware of what information about themselves is revealed through their own use of language. For example, questions that mask autobiographical or self statements ('Shouldn't you first sort out your feelings toward your father?') should be examined. It may well be that it is the counsellor, and not the client, who has a need to examine his familial relationships. If the autobiographical content of such statements arise out of the counsellor's own situation rather than the client's, they need to be recognised and dealt with in ways that are appropriate to the needs of the client.

EXERCISE 3.10

1 Ask close friends and other counsellors to describe what they see as your typical verbal and behavioural mannerisms. Find out how they react to those habits. Which ones would you want to alter and why?

2 On audio or video, tape a series of counselling role plays or actual counselling sessions. Replay them and note your verbal and behavioural habits. Ask others to comment on the effect they seem to have on your clients. Which ones would you want to alter and why?

Engaging reluctant clients
This section has been adapted from an article by R.J. Manthei and D.A. Matthews. [*Helping the reluctant client to engage in counselling*, British Journal of Guidance and Counselling, *1982*, 10, *pp. 44–50: CRAC/Hobsons Press, Bateman St., Cambridge CB2 1LZ, England.*] Reluctant or resistant clients are part of every counsellor's experience. Faced with reluctant clients, counsellors can choose to accept their reluctance at face value, ie, as an unequivocal refusal of help. Alternatively, they can sensitively and non-judgementally attempt to engage the client so that the real meaning of the reluctance may become clear. Many reluctant clients may need only to find genuineness, reassurance, and the right invitation from a counsellor to begin a relationship. When working with such clients, it is essential to allow them time to feel comfortable and develop trust, to refrain from pre-judging clients' moods, motives, and needs, and to try out more than the normal variety of invitations to talk or participate.

INTERPRETING THE CLIENT'S SILENCE

Initially, confronted with a client's silence, the counsellor should try to assess what the silence means for the client, and some of the reasons for the behaviour.

Silence can express many things: anger, fear, boredom, respect, embarrassment, sadness, contempt. Counsellors should make every attempt to understand the possible meanings of silence. In doing this, particular attention should be paid to the client's movements, gestures, and physical appearance. Commenting on these things can result in the client agreeing with or correcting the observation. Either way, the client has been engaged.

Interpreting clients' feelings can be accomplished by written means. For example, clients may respond to a written observation or a simple drawing. When using written messages, counsellors should write simply and briefly, in large letters and in full view of the client.

Mirroring as a form of interpretation can be used to highlight dominant aspects of a client's behaviour. In this technique, counsellors imitate movements, gestures, or postures that seem meaningful. Mirroring can be a provocative form of interpretation and may elicit a strong response, positive or negative.

ENCOURAGING NON-VERBAL RESPONDING

These techniques are intended to encourage the client to initiate exploration and self-disclosure without having to verbalise thoughts and feelings.

It is often effective to invite clients to draw or write thoughts or feelings they find hard to verbalise.

Clients can be encouraged to express thoughts physically: eg, by acting, miming, or posturing. Almost any verbal message can be communicated physically in a way that makes the meaning more clear and direct.

Having once engaged clients to act out thoughts or feelings, counsellors should ask them to exaggerate specific behaviours. Repeating a gesture with emphasised movement may aid a client to clarify its meaning and the personal feelings that lie behind it.

WORKING AT THE CLIENT'S PACE

Many counsellors, pressed by time and institutional demands, quickly become frustrated with reluctant clients. In some cases dealing with the reluctance indirectly will foster trust and the development of an appropriate relationship.

Counsellors should try taking reluctant clients for a walk; giving them some small non-counselling task to do; allowing them to remain while the counsellor continues with other work. The client may simply need time to get to know and trust the counsellor enough to begin talking.

Clients can be asked to bring photographs of self, family, or friends, that they are willing to share. Some of the techniques described earlier can then be used to comment on and interpret the photograph.

If clients are agreeable, they can be given some small bit of 'homework' to perform before the next session. They may be curious, and co-operate long enough to see what the counsellor has in mind.

The counsellor can try changing seating positions and/or activities. In some cases a mere change of position or activity will result in a client being more willing to interact.

RESPONDING TO THE TALKATIVE RELUCTANT CLIENT

Some reluctant clients will readily verbalise feelings such as hostility and anger, or interact in over-compliant or evasive ways. The effect is the same: avoidance of meaningful contact with the counsellor.

As in the case of the silent client, counsellors should pay particular attention to the talkative client's movements, gestures, and physical appearance.

The manner in which a client speaks may reveal as much as what is actually said. Counsellors should be sensitive to voice quality and use such information in responding.

In many instances it will be productive to have clients repeat particular statements, phrases, or words. This repetition can serve to highlight underlying feelings and to clarify meanings.

If video tape equipment is available, clients can be asked to view themselves and comment on what they see.

EXPLAINING THE COUNSELLING PROCESS

In some cases, clients' reluctance to engage in counselling can be largely overcome by explaining the counselling process, how it works, and what the client can expect from the counsellor. The mere fact that counsellors are prepared to reveal their motives, intentions, thoughts, and feelings can act as an incentive and model for the client to do likewise.

These suggestions indicate the range of counsellor behaviours that could be used if the reluctant or difficult client is approached with patience, open-mindedness, sensitivity, and creativity.

Counsellors should be aware of the possibility that generally co-operative clients may show reluctance when certain topics are introduced. Counsellors should also remember that they do not have the right to persist in efforts to engage unwilling clients in talk. Reluctance may show something more than a temporary reticence. It may indicate a message that should be heeded: Leave me alone. In the face of marked resistance the counsellor should try referring the client elsewhere or simply end the contact. The counsellor should regard these as appropriate moves and not necessarily as signs of personal failure.

Thinking aloud
Occasionally a client says something that leads the counsellor to believe that a shift in topic could be productive. Rather than making a seemingly abrupt change which may leave the client puzzled or irritated, the counsellor should think aloud.

For example:

During a vocational interview a client interested in medical laboratory work for which there are limited vacancies, reveals that her school subjects are English, mathematics, physics, chemistry, and biology. The counsellor may then inquire whether the client has ever considered careers in commerce. Lest this switch seem inexplicable, the counsellor could think aloud, something like this:

'There are limited vacancies in medical laboratory work. I wonder whether you have ever considered careers in commerce. It is possible to take these up without having studied commercial subjects at school. Your maths is strong and could be used in accounting or data processing.'

The skill of thinking aloud has two specific uses: (a) to explain to the client what is happening in the counselling process, and (b) to explain the reason for a sudden change in topic. In the first instance the counsellor's aim is to allay a client's doubt, hesitation, or suspicion about what is happening. Usually a short, clear explanation will reassure the client and help her to make sense of what is going on.

For example:

'I need to know some specific information about your son's

medical condition before we discuss further the ways in which his behaviour is disruptive at home.'

'We will spend the first part of this hour discussing your job likes and dislikes, and then I will have you complete a short job-interest inventory that should help us to focus our discussion on specific job types.'

Immediacy

Immediacy is recognising what is going on between the counsellor and the client at a particular moment and communicating this constructively. Because this communication usually refers to feelings, it can be very powerful, and it may be threatening to a client who is unused to intimate, honest communication. Therefore, it should be done tentatively and expressed only as an opinion. It indicates that the counsellor accepts the person sufficiently to be completely open about their interaction.

For example:

'I'm feeling that maybe you are becoming irritated with me right now.'

'I feel that perhaps you're reluctant to be here.'

Using silence

We are often afraid of, or embarrassed by, silences during conversations. Silences, however, may be as revealing as the spoken word. Acceptance of a client's silence may emphasise to her that it is her right to determine the nature of the interview. It allows both counsellor and client time to think. It builds trust and may eventually encourage the client to be very frank in her revelations.

To use silence effectively the counsellor needs to accept its worth, to feel confident about allowing it to continue, and to be sensitive to timing. If possible, the counsellor should let the client be the first to break the silence. If, however, the silence seems to convey a strong sense of resentment on the part of the client, especially an involuntary one, it can be helpful to verbalise this and invite the client to leave if she wishes.

EXERCISE 3.11

1 When replaying a video or audio tape of one of your interviews, note whenever: a new topic was introduced, you thought aloud, you used immediacy, you used silence.
   (a) Note what happened immediately before your use of each skill.
   (b) Note the effect of using each skill.

2 Alternatively, during role-playing or actual interviews, an observer could be asked to note these things for you.

Identifying feelings

The ability to perceive and respond accurately to another person's feelings is essential if the counsellor is to help that person talk about what is on her mind or underlying her difficulties. Counsellors must be sensitive to more than just the content of a client's message. Very often the way in which the client speaks is more important than the words she uses to express herself.

Responding to feeling is a powerful technique because of its intimacy and the fact that, more than most other counsellor behaviours, it communicates acceptance of and empathy with the client. In normal social interactions, feelings are regularly disguised and controlled. Thus, when someone perceives our feelings accurately, it tends to have a profound effect on us. We usually react positively to the person who has understood us, and we realise that our feelings, whatever they might be, are justified.

Read the following:

Client: I've had it! She always does that to me and I hate it!
Counsellor: Could it be that you're partly to blame?
Client: I've had it! She always does that to me and I hate it!
Counsellor: You really seem angry about this.

Note the difference in the responses. The first deals only with the content of what was said and asks an emotional person to look at her situation rationally. The second recognises the person's feeling state and implies that the feeling is acceptable and has been understood. Think of a similar situation you have been in. What is the effect on you when someone accepts what you have said – words, feeling and all?

The first requirement for dealing with feelings in a counselling situation is to be able to recognise when feelings are being communicated. The counsellor should encourage the client to specify and identify what she feels; he should not rely solely on his own interpretation of what the client might be feeling, no matter how obvious the feeling might appear to be. The counsellor can simply and effectively clarify this by asking some variation of the following:

'How does that make you feel?
'What are you feeling right now?'

EXERCISE 3.12*

This exercise, adapted from one by John L. Wallen and D.W. Johnson [*D.W. Johnson*, Reaching Out, *Englewood Cliffs, N.J. Prentice Hall, 1972.*], is designed to highlight the difference between statements that describe exactly how the speaker feels and those that are merely emotional without describing the specific feeling involved.

For each of the following items there are three statements. Only one actually describes a feeling; the others may *contain* or *imply* feeling but do not specifically *describe* the feeling involved. Select the statement that most directly *describes* the speaker's feeling.

1 (a) 'I feel you are always picking on me.'
  (b) 'Leave me alone!'
  (c) 'It angers me when you always blame me.'
2 (a) 'I began to feel depressed when Jill and I broke up. After that nothing seemed to go right.'
  (b) 'I feel things haven't been going right lately, ever since Jill and I broke up.'
  (c) 'Anyone would feel less than his best if he had just lost his girlfriend.'
3 (a) 'My reaction to that assignment was pretty definite.'
  (b) 'Would you like it if you had to do all that work?'
  (c) 'It's not fair that we have to do this. I'm pretty mad about it.'
4 (a) 'I'm afraid about what you've stirred up by talking to my parents.'
  (b) 'I feel that you have really ruined things for me.'
  (c) 'Why did you have to tell my parents? Anybody should know better than to do that.'
5 (a) 'I feel you know a lot about things. I wish I could say that about myself'.
  (b) 'You interest me.'
  (c) 'When you talk, I feel relieved because I know I'm not the only person who feels this way.'
6 (a) 'This is an interesting exercise.'
  (b) 'I really feel challenged by this exercise.'
  (c) 'I'm sure everyone liked doing this exercise.'

Expressing feelings
The measure of a counsellor's success in working with feelings in a counselling situation is largely determined by his ability to

recognise his own feelings as they occur and to use them in a manner that is most helpful to the client. Using feelings effectively can mean a number of things. When the counsellor openly shares his feelings with a client, he may be modelling desirable behaviour or enhancing a climate of trust and honesty. Similarly, open expression of feelings can relieve interpersonal tensions and demonstrate to clients that feelings themselves need not be overwhelming or disabling. Even when not directly communicated to the client, the counsellor's feelings can be used constructively. For example, once the counsellor recognises a feeling within himself, he should next determine whether it is the direct result of his interaction with the client or whether it arises out of his own personal experience. In both instances the counsellor can make constructive use of his feelings beyond merely expressing them to the client. The counsellor responses below illustrate this.

1 'I feel good when you say that. I appreciate being told when I have been helpful.'
2 'No, I'm not happy to talk to you either. But, now that ·we're both here, what are we going to do?'
3 'I'm feeling annoyed by your constant apologies for things. I wonder if others might have the same reaction?'
4 (Thinking to himself): 'I'm nervous. Why? I'm never comfortable when sitting this close to another person.' (To client); 'I'm going to move back slightly so I can be a bit more relaxed.'

In the first response the counsellor is demonstrating how to receive a compliment by simply accepting it without modifying or discounting it. The second response models and enhances interpersonal honesty (the counsellor does not pretend he is glad to see this reluctant client) and may relieve tension by openly sharing negative feelings. In the third response the counsellor expresses a negative reaction to his client but does so in a way that encourages the client to take a closer look at how she may affect others. The counsellor's nervousness in the fourth response arises out of his own experience, but by simply stating what he is going to do and why, his actions becomes constructive in the sense that it models direct, open communication.

Feelings should be dealt with as they arise in counselling. The counsellor should be continually aware of how he is feeling and what has caused these feelings. Likewise, the client should be continually encouraged to express and explore her feelings. If feelings remain unspoken, they may dominate the relationship and inhibit a more rational approach to a problem. Often merely recognising and expressing a feeling is enough to lessen it, control it, accept it, or shift one's attention from it.

Think of a situation in which you were very angry. Of the following, which would you prefer to have had said to you? Why?

1 'You know, this whole thing might not be as bad as you think.'
2 'This whole business has really made you mad!'

EXERCISE 3.13

1 Take part in a role-play using short client statements that are designed to provoke some feeling in the counsellor. The following client statements are given as examples:
   (a) 'You never say anything! You just sit there nodding and saying "yes" all the time. I thought you were going to help me!'
   (b) 'You're so easy to talk to. You seem to understand everything I say and do. I just know you will do something for me.'
   (c) 'You lied. You said that what we talked about here was just between us, but this morning the teacher asked me if I had talked to you yet. You had no right to tell him I was coming.'
   (d) 'What's the matter with you? I've said I don't know but you don't seem to believe me. If I knew what to do, I wouldn't be here.'
   (e) 'Leave me alone. (Long silence) . . .
   The counsellor role-player should respond to each client statement by identifying his own feeling reaction to the client. For example, the counsellor may feel hurt or guilty or even angry in response to client statement (a) above.
2 When the counsellor is quickly and accurately able to recognise the feelings within himself, he should write a constructive response and then discuss it with the client role-player to determine its effect. The counsellor may write something like the following in response to statement (a) above: 'You're mad and confused about what I'm doing. How would you like me to act?'
3 Finally, individuals make up client statements of their own. Teachers, counsellors, social workers, and probation officers can use situations that are typical of their own work. The statements can be audio or video taped if such equipment is available. This allows the same material to be used on several occasions.

EXERCISE 3.14

As you do the exercises in this book, note your feelings and reactions. As often as possible stop working, identify your feeling and express it either in writing or orally. For example, you may feel foolish or irritated, excited or pleased. Write or say what you feel, such as: 'I feel nervous about role-playing in front of a group.' By doing this you will become more aware of your present feelings and will be able to express them more accurately and quickly.

Reflection
Effective use of reflection conveys to the client that the counsellor is trying to understand what she has said, that he has understood correctly and that he accepts her. A counsellor can reflect content by a short, simple re-statement or paraphrasing of the essence of what the client has actually said. Reflection of content condenses and crystallises in a fresh way the information a client gives. The counsellor can also reflect feeling, that part of the client's statement that represents the emotional message. Often what is said (content) does not communicate the real meaning. Reflection of feeling focuses on this underlying or unstated message.

Reflection should be used to demonstrate understanding, but more importantly, to facilitate the client's movement toward more complete self-awareness and self-understanding. It is appropriate and effective to use reflection skills at any stage of the counselling process.

For example:
Client: I don't think I could do it. I'd only fail. I . . . well – I've never been able to get grades like that before and I'm sure I couldn't now.
Counsellor: (content reflection) Your past records convince you it's not possible now.
(feeling reflection) You're feeling a bit afraid to even try.

EXERCISE 3.15

In the following exercise there are four client statements. After each one write (a) the counsellor response that best reflects the content of the statement, and (b) the response that best reflects feeling, ie, the response which indicates that you understand the client's attitude and the situation as it appears to her.

Compare and discuss your answers with others doing the same exercise.

1 'No, I won't! I'm not going to tell you any of my business. I didn't ask to see you. I was sent! You're not getting anything out of me!

2 'I really need your help. I just can't seem to make friends with any decent kids. They just ignore me and – I don't know – I just feel – I'm wondering is there something wrong with me? Do *you* think there's something wrong with me?'

3 'Nearly two more years! Honestly I just couldn't stand two more years of school. Oh, I can do it all right – I know I can pass the exams. But it's all so boring! I'm changing my mind about going to university.'

4 'Well, OK, it *is* at home. But what difference does it make talking to you about it? You wouldn't understand. You just don't know what it's like there day after day.'

EXERCISE 3.16

Next time you are listening to an interview on a television or radio current events programme, notice how often the interviewer reflects the *feeling* of the person being interviewed as opposed to the *content* of what has been said. What seems to be the effect of each type of reflection on the person interviewed?

Accurate understanding

In counselling it is necessary to understand what the client is saying and to be able to communicate your understanding to her. Understanding involves far more than merely hearing the words that are spoken. It necessitates careful listening to, and awareness of, all the verbal and non-verbal aspects of what the client is communicating. The counsellor must rely on his perceptions of the client and his 'hunches' about what is going on, but at the same time be careful not to interpret what he *thinks* the client has said nor take her for granted.

Effective listening, like other skills, can be practised. When practising, be aware of the following considerations:

1 Be aware of your attitude. How do you feel about the client and how are those feelings influencing you perceptions of her?

2 Be attentive both to what is being said (content) and what is implied or hinted at (unstated or emotional message).

3 Focus on what the other person is trying to tell you, not on what you might say in response or how you can straighten out the mix-up.

4 Listening involves not only immediate understanding, but also clarifying what is obscure. Do not hesitate to say that you do not fully understand. Also, do not assume anything about your client. Ask, even if the answer seems very obvious.

Practising understanding involves 'perception-checking' which simply means that the counsellor asks the client how accurate his listening has been. The effect of perception-checking is to demonstrate interest, understanding, and an openness of mind.

EXERCISE 3.17

Following is a list of counsellor responses or leads that can be used to see if you understood correctly. They are included to give you some ideas of how this skill can be implemented.

> Is what you're saying . .
> You seem to be saying . . .
> You feel . . .
> As you see it . . .
> Let me see if I understood correctly. You . . ., is that right?
> Am I correct in assuming that you . . .
> From your point of view . . .
> What I hear you saying is . . .
> Correct me if I'm wrong, but . . .

Using short client statements (see exercise 3.13), counsellors could use leads like those listed above to check their understanding of what has been said. In addition, the following client statements may be used for counsellors to practise accurate understanding.

(a) 'I think I can do it, but sometimes I don't know. Anyway, I guess it's worth a try.'
(b) 'I'm not sure how I feel. Sometimes I'm angry about failing; other times I just don't care. But it does bother me.'
(c) Client sits quietly, looking sad.
(d) 'I've got to get help. If you don't do something, I'll never get started.'
(e) 'Things are fine now. Thanks. I guess you won't want to see me next week.'

1 Counsellors should write their responses and then discuss them with the other members of the group to make sure that each response shows that the counsellor is trying to understand. For

example, the counsellor might write the following in response to client statement (a):

'You don't sound as though you really want to try. Is that right?'

2 When counsellors are able to write effective responses quickly and accurately, they should respond orally. Again, the responses should be discussed, so that each counsellor is sure that his was an effective understanding check.

3 Individuals can make up client statements of their own to suit their particular work or personal situations.

EXERCISE 3.18

When listening to a dialogue or interview on television or radio, count the number of times the interviewer uses perception-checking to clarify his understanding of what the other person has said.

4
Developing the problem-solving process

We now move to the skills involved in the second and third stages of the problem-solving sequence – goal setting and strategy selection.

THE SKILLS OF GOAL SETTING

Direct questioning
As the name implies, direct questioning is the skill of focusing the discussion on a specific point. It is used to help clarify an issue the counsellor feels would be worth exploring further. This skill should be used sparingly until the client has been given ample opportunity to examine his situation at his own pace and in his own manner. When used, the direct question or probing question should be open rather than closed. This allows the client maximum freedom to respond and keeps the counsellor from appearing to be an interrogator.

1 *Client:* Gavin didn't keep his promise to me.
   Counsellor: (closed) Did you try reminding him of it?
   (open) How does that affect your relationship with him?
2 *Client:* Mum's OK. We get along fine. She seems to understand me. Dad's all right too, I guess.
   Counsellor: You don't seem too sure about Dad. How do you get along with him?

Dealing with discrepancies*

Dealing with discrepancies involves the skill of honestly and directly pointing out to the client that his description of himself or his situation clearly does not match the way in which the counsellor sees the same situation. It is a skill that is initiated by the counsellor and is an expression of her own point of view rather than simply an explanation or interpretation based on one of the client's views. Discrepant behaviours can involve such things as strengths or weaknesses a client refuses to acknowledge, misinformation or lack of information, reluctance to put a stated intention into action, or a refusal to try to see another point of view.

When pointing out a discrepancy to a client, the counsellor should focus on present feelings and behaviour and not on what the client has said or done in the past. To use this skill effectively, a counsellor must be able to:

(a) Recognise her own feelings as they occur.
(b) State those feelings clearly and simply.
(c) Tell the client her honest reaction to the behaviour or statement and the specific reasons for that reaction.
(d) Allow the client the opportunity to respond to that reaction.

Highlighting discrepancies involves risk, but if successful, it can greatly hasten the counselling process or overcome a block or barrier. If a helping relationship has already been developed, pointing out a discrepancy is less risky and may in fact be seen as challenging and helpful by the client. One way of highlighting a discrepancy is to use the sentence form: 'On the one hand, you . . . and yet on the other hand, you . . . Can you explain that contradiction?'

1 'You say constantly that you are going to get up on time and get to school, but you never do.'
2 'You keep saying you love your wife, but you don't seem to want to make her happier by staying home more often.'

---

*In previous editions of this book the skill of dealing with discrepancies was labelled 'confrontation'. We have changed the label to avoid the tendency to equate confrontation with conflict, tension, and even antagonism between the client and counsellor. Dealing with discrepancies is a more neutral term and more accurately describes the intent of the skill.

3 'Right now I hear you saying things are getting better, but you have been mistaken about that twice before. What's different about this time?'

EXERCISE 4.1

1 Form groups of three. In each group decide who will first be counsellor, who will be client and who will be observer. The counsellor and client are to role-play the first situation given below. The counsellor is to identify any discrepancy that appears in what the client has been doing or saying. The observer should make sure that the counsellor does point out a discrepancy and does so in a way that allows the client some freedom to respond.

2 When finished, each person should swap roles and repeat the above procedure until each has had a chance to function as counsellor.

Role-play 1: You suspect the client is experiencing sexual problems in his marriage because, although the client insists there are no problems in this area, he refuses to discuss any aspect of sex and always manages to change the subject when you bring it up.

Role-play 2: The client insists he wants to change his critical and sarcastic way with people but he consistently refuses to discuss specific ways of altering this behaviour.

Role-play 3: The client keeps making negative statements about his artistic talents in spite of a number of compliments from others and praise from his art instructor.

EXERCISE 4.2

Think of some situation in your own life in which you could have benefitted from having a discrepancy pointed out to you. Write a statement in which you deal with that discrepancy. Choose another person with whom to share your statement. As you do this, try to be aware of how you are feeling as you do it and why.

Setting goals

Some clients express their goals in vague general terms. In the behaviour-change phase of counselling the first job of the counsellor is to get her client to be clear and specific about his goals. She may do this by helping him to break a general goal into smaller more manageable ones, to plan practical steps towards a goal, or to choose one main goal from a number of desired ones.

A useful technique to assist goal setting is to encourage the client to think of alternative ways of behaving. This forces him to be practical. For example, the counsellor could ask, 'What do you want to do differently?' or, 'You're getting upset at the way your children react to you. What would you like them to do instead?' Answers may come in the form of goals such as these: 'Have more fun with the children.' 'Be able to study better.' 'Avoid nagging.'

Helpful though these goals are, each should be made still more precise. 'More fun with the children' might come to be defined in several different ways — having a game with them for at least 20 minutes every day, or swapping a joke every morning, or reading a story every evening. The goal of 'more effective study' might be specified as reading and taking notes without a break for 40 minutes at least twice a day. Negative goals such as 'stop nagging' need to be put in positive terms, so that there is something definite to aim for. 'Stop nagging' might then be changed into making a request pleasantly, very specifically, with careful timing, and once only.

Exercise 4.3*

1 Label each of the following as either 'G' (a general goal) or 'S' (a specific behaviour): (a) playing poker; (b) being a good conversationalist; (c) feeling on top of the world; (d) asking open-ended questions; (e) improving work habits; (f) relaxing in the evening; (g) inviting two friends to lunch; (h) driving the car; (i) feeling competent; (j) standing no nonsense; (k) doing yoga for 5 minutes daily; (l) setting the table. Check the answers at the end of the book and discuss them with others.
2 Write a specific goal for each of these general goals: (a) losing weight; (b) improving my appearance; (c) standing up to my mother; (d) getting fit; (e) not boring other people; (f) controlling the class better; (g) getting on top of the job; (h) taking a break. For each goal, list the behaviours suggested by the group.

Supporting and encouraging
Used skilfully, support and encouragement of the client as a person who is accepted and capable of coping, can be extremely reassuring and energising. Much of the feeling of support and encouragement may be conveyed non-verbally through eye contact, facial expression, smiling, posture, touch, and tone of voice.

When using verbal means to convey support and encouragement, the counsellor should affirm the whole person rather than judge particular beliefs, attitudes, and behaviour. If the counsellor's responses merely show approval of particular aspects of the person, there is the risk of being judgemental about what is good or bad, right or wrong for the client.

Note the differences between these three counsellor responses. Which is least judgemental and why? Which is the most obviously influencing or persuading?

Client: I have really worked at changing and I think I'm finally getting somewhere.

Counsellor:

(a) That sounds great! That's what I was hoping to hear.

(b) You sound more positive now. I'm glad to hear it.

(c) I knew you could do it; never doubted it for a minute.

Interpretation

Interpretations are explanations of, or insights into, a situation. When used in counselling, they should help a client to understand the meaning of events by presenting alternative views of his problem. Interpretations will be more helpful if they arise from information the client presents rather than from the counsellor's experience and theoretical knowledge.

The counsellor should remember that an interpretation is merely one possible explanation of an event. Her client may have entirely different and equally valid explanations. The counsellor should offer interpretations tentatively, allowing the client sufficient opportunity to modify them.

Read the following counsellor interpretations. Both are based on what the client has previously said and both offer him the chance to reject or modify his statement.

1 'From what you have said about your father, it seems that you are really very frightened of him. Is that how you see it?'

2 'You sound as if you're extremely embarrassed about being overweight. Perhaps your aggressiveness toward others is an attempt to cover your shame. Could that be right?'

Interpretation, like many of the other leading behaviours, can have negative aspects. It can be an impersonal technique that emphasises the superior status of the counsellor. Also, too often clients will accept interpretations as factual, fatalistic explanations and cease working to change things. Offering interpretations can be valuable and necessary in counselling, but presenting them as final explanations serves only to satisfy a counsellor need, not a client need. Finally, it is our belief that a counsellor's effectiveness should never be measured by the ingeniousness or frequency of her interpretations.

EXERCISE 4.4

1 Think of how you felt at some point today. Try to think of as many interpretations of these feelings as you can. For example, you might begin by remembering that you felt annoyed at being misunderstood. Then try to think of all the possible explanations for that feeling (eg., 'She asked for my opinion but then didn't really seem interested – I felt foolish trying to explain.')
2 Which explanation seems to be the best? Why?

EXERCISE 4.5

1 Write down as many possible explanations or interpretations as you can for the first client statement below. Then discuss your interpretations with others to find out which ones satisfy the requirements of an effective interpretation (eg, based on what the client has said or directly implied, adds new meaning to the situation, presented in a way that allows the client to reject or modify it).
   (a) 'I've really messed things up with that teacher. I hate the class, the work, her. I'm really worried about my attitude.'
   (b) 'I'm finished. That factory job is too dull . . . I'm sick of putting the same piece in each crate hour after hour. I'm tired, bored, unhappy . . .'
2 Using the second client statement, respond orally with as many interpretations as you and others can think of. Discuss them to make sure they are effective interpretations.

Giving information
There are many times when simply giving required information is the most useful thing to do. If a client asks for factual information that is directly relevant to his problem, it should be clearly, promptly, and simply given.

Beginning counsellors, having learned to be wary of giving information, are sometimes reluctant to answer direct questions. They feel they should not answer until they are absolutely certain that the 'real' problem has been identified. Thus, they may be evasive and tend to probe beyond what the client has already revealed. This behaviour is irritating and confusing to the client.

Another situation that causes counsellors difficulty is when a client asks them direct, personal questions. Again, in most cases a direct, simple answer is best, even if it is a refusal to divulge the information. Clients will be more confused by and suspicious of a hesitant, evasive, or equivocal reply than they will a direct refusal.

Below are examples of giving information and handling direct client questions.

1 *Client:* Has my maths teacher talked to you about me yet?
   Counsellor: No. If *you'd* like to talk to me, though, you may.
2 *Client:* What do you think I should do?
   Counsellor: Well, I don't really know. I wonder what you *want* me to say.
3 *Client:* Have you ever smoked pot?
   Counsellor: Yes, I tried it once.

In the first example, the counsellor gives a simple, negative answer to the client's question and then invites him to talk about what is on his mind. An alternative response could have been, 'No. What would the maths teacher want to talk to me about?' This is more direct and possibly more threatening to the client but potentially as effective. It is often useful to follow your direct response to the client's question with an invitation to talk or with an open question about the client's feelings or beliefs. For instance, in the second example the counsellor avoids making a decision for the client and then invites him to explore his own preferences. In the third example, the counsellor merely answers the client without any explanation and waits to see what the client's next response will be.

Giving advice

We believe advice should be given as little as possible; only when requested, and only after careful listening has ensured that the counsellor understands the client's situation. It is a skill that is easily misused. Advice-giving is open to game-playing in that it places the counsellor in the role of expert (and all experts are sooner or later proved wrong). Also, it may be a manoeuvre by the client to avoid taking responsibility for himself or to avoid looking at an issue fully.

When advice is given, try to base it on reasons the client has previously offered in support of one particular option over others. When this is not possible, the counsellor should state the reasons why she feels a particular option is better for the client than the other options. Seeing things from this new perspective may then at least give the client feedback about himself.

Client: Even after all our talking I can't decide which to take, biology or art.

Counsellor: Well, why don't you try art. You're already taking two sciences this year, you say you want to explore other fields and you like the art teacher.

Sometimes the counsellor can use advice-giving to help a client make a decision. There are times when a counsellor suspects that a client who professes to be undecided actually prefers one option over the others. When this situation arises, the client's preference becomes obvious (through verbal and non-verbal signs) as soon as the counsellor purposely advises another course of action. This type of advice-giving should be used sparingly and only after the counsellor fully understands the client's situation.

Influencing

The counsellor uses these responses in an attempt to change the client's beliefs, attitudes, or behaviour. There are times when it seems that all the client needs is a 'push' to get started or make a decision. However, when used too frequently or without a complete understanding of the client's situation, attempts to persuade will usually be unsuccessful. The counsellor also risks disappointment if she too confidently believes that she knows what is best for the client, and then the client chooses another course of action. Like advice-giving, influencing is open to game-playing in that any failure can be blamed on the counsellor for offering the wrong solution.

Client: It's no use. I just don't feel comfortable in that situation.

Counsellor:

  (a) I'm sure you can do it, especially if you follow the way we practised it here.

  (b) If you don't, I'm afraid I can't help you any more.

Note the difference between the two counsellor responses. When would each be most effective and why?

Giving directions

An obvious, but essential skill in helping clients to act or to change is the ability to give simple, clear directions or suggestions, using language the client understands. Giving clients precise directions can occur at any stage of the counselling process but is most often used when helping someone to practise a new behaviour or initiate change. For example, while some clients might readily respond to 'Close your eyes and go with the energy flow', others may respond more readily to 'Close your eyes, sit in a position that feels relaxed, and just let your thoughts come and go. Do not try to control them'. In order to be effective, directions and suggestions must be brief, understandable, and perceived by the client to be relevant to the subject of discussion.

Exercise 4.6

As counsellor, give clear, simple directions so that the client can:
(a) Play the role of his angry mother.
(b) Adopt a more assertive posture.

Using personal examples

Sometimes it seems that it would be reassuring and supportive to a client to hear that the counsellor has experienced a similar situation and what she did to cope with it. However, we would again urge caution in using this skill. It is our experience that we have almost always regretted using personal examples. They take the focus off the client and detract from his feeling of being most important and central in the relationship. Think of a situation in which you were describing something of importance to you, and another person began telling of a similar experience of their own. How did you feel?

The example below illustrates three necessary aspects of an effective personal anecdote: it should be succinct; it should be relevant to the client's concern; and the focus of the interview should quickly move back to the client.

Client: I just can't face a group. I get nervous and forget what I am supposed to say.

Counsellor: Yes, I know that feeling well. I was so frightened of groups it almost kept me from becoming a teacher. But I'm sure that if we work on it, you can overcome your fear.

Advising a delay

Sometimes it is prudent and effective to advise the client to delay making a decision, in effect to make no decision for a period of time. This is especially so when (a) important information about the concern will become available in a few days (eg, a student's decision to continue with a course of study will be better made after the midyear exam results are made known next week); (b) the client is unrealistically panicky about things and feeling pushed to make a hasty decision (eg, the client, a high school student, feels it is time he was more decisive and that to satisfy his parents he should decide immediately what subjects he will study at university next year); and (c) the problem has been exaggerated beyond what is realistic (eg, a man whose write-up of a project at work was criticised has decided that he has no future with the company and should quit his job immediately).

In most of these situations delaying the decision-making allows the client to gather more information about the situation, to become more clear about an attendant issue or concern, or to clarify what the problem or concern actually involves. Convincing the client to delay deciding can be problematic: in many instances delaying a decision will have to be presented to him as a positive, decisive act. For example, it may be possible to prioritise specific steps in the decision-making so that finding out how he did on midyear exams becomes the first, necessary step in deciding whether to continue a course of study (see (a) above).

Gaining commitment

The client's motivation to change his behaviour is a major factor in counselling. It is best if he chooses and specifies his own goal, for he is then more likely to work hard to achieve it. But a counsellor who has developed a good working relationship with a client should not hesitate to offer suggestions as a way of prompting his thinking. She should ensure, however, that he commits himself fully to his goal and that he accepts responsibility for it. If the counsellor neglects to do this, the client may blame her for any failure. The counsellor should take care that the client commits himself to a goal that he sees as being realistic and desirable, and one into which he is prepared to put time and effort.

In getting such a commitment from the client, several of the earlier skills will be important. The skill of influencing might be needed to convince those who give up easily and who express fatalistic attitudes, saying, 'It's just hereditary — my mother was exactly the same.' Without pushing too hard, the counsellor should give one or two carefully chosen examples, using ordinary language and citing details that seem close to her situation: 'Many parents have been able to stop children's temper tantrums in just a week or so, and without getting upset themselves.'

Sometimes a client's reactions to a counsellor's attempt to get him to specify goals might contradict his stated aims. In such a case pointing out a discrepancy might be an appropriate technique: 'You tell me that you want to be able to talk to your girl-friend on more equal terms, but you still haven't come up with any topic that you're willing to start on, and you've objected to every suggestion I've made.' Obviously, the success of such a response by the counsellor will depend upon her having established an open and honest relationship with her client earlier.

The counsellor might find it helpful to formalise an agreement beyond the client's oral statement. If a client finds it very difficult to bring himself to act in a certain situation, asking him to write down his plan in simple direct language could be useful. He could even be asked to sign and date a written statement or contract, for example: 'I agree to practise how I will enter the room, sit down, move about, present myself, and talk to the group. I will do this three times this week just before each meeting. After each meeting I will write down all the things I did well and also those things I still need to work on. I will bring this record to the next session and talk about it.'

Notice that this contract sets out:

1 Exactly what the client is to do.
2 How often he will do it.
3 How it will be used at the next session.

Such contracts should be planned jointly by the counsellor and her client. Provided that the task is relevant to his problem and is realistic and simple, then carrying it out will be satisfying to him. It is important that the client is motivated and actively participates in changing his behaviour. Requiring him to plan and execute tasks in this way ensures his involvement.

EXERCISE 4.7

1 Role-play in counsellor/client pairs. The client's role is to express doubts about being able to do certain things. Assume that the client has little formal education. Give the exact words you would use to convince him that it is possible to learn to:
(a) Stop children's temper tantrums.
(b) Ask for help from a welfare agency.
(c) Refuse overtime work.
(d) Make a complaint to a teacher.
(e) Ask that something borrowed be returned.
(f) Return unsatisfactory goods to a shop.
(g) Ask for a small favour.
(h) Cut short a boring conversation.
2 In pairs plan a contract which follows the three basic rules. Choose any topics, eg, a physical fitness programme, a new way of doing a routine chore.

THE SKILLS OF STRATEGY SELECTION

Anticipating situations

Having gained her client's commitment to a precise goal, the counsellor's next job is to help him plan exactly how, when, and where the change process will start in earnest. He should be made aware of the many factors that contribute to success. Among these is the importance of first practising only in those situations in which the chances of success are very good.

Everything should be planned carefully. He should be helped to choose the best time and place to start, to decide exactly what to say and do, to imagine how he wants to look and feel, to consider likely reactions of others, and of himself, and to anticipate his response to these different reactions. Such matters should be fully discussed so that the client feels very secure in what he is planning to do. The counsellor should encourage him to anticipate success, even if it might be unpleasant for him to think about the situation beforehand.

The prospect of failure should also be discussed, because it would be foolish of the counsellor to guarantee success. While the emphasis should be on the positive aspects and on planning for success, the client should be encouraged to think of failure as 'nothing lost', and as an opportunity to make better plans for the next occasion.

EXERCISE 4.8

Write out a detailed plan to handle each of the following tasks. In each case try to anticipate what could possibly happen and work out a plan to deal with each (eg, If he says this, I'll say that):

1 Declining an invitation that you expect to be given face-to-face and in a very pressing manner.
2 Expressing first your doubts about, then your firm opposition to, something you had previously agreed to.
3 Talking in an interview with a domineering supervisor about two aspects of your job that you want to see altered.

Discuss each plan with a partner.

Providing models

Modelling means providing a good example or pattern of behaviour for the client who does not know how to act appropriately in some situation. At one level, of course, modelling could mean simply showing a physical example, eg, a client's note-taking might be improved by seeing a sample page done by a fellow student. Counsellors should be alert to opportunities for helping clients in such simple ways.

Usually, however, modelling refers to actions which seem very complicated but which do not result in a product like a page of notes. For this reason modelling is commonly demonstrated in two ways – both completely, without a break, to show the total effect, and also in segments so that the separate skills can be isolated for observation and practice. The counsellor can act as a model in her office. A peer or colleague of the client can act as a model for him in the client's ordinary social setting. A model can also take the form of a special presentation of the behaviour, eg, film or video tape.

There are some obvious advantages and disadvantages to these alternatives. The most serious disadvantage is that the performance of the peer or colleague cannot be controlled or repeated. It is best if the counsellor can emphasise the vital parts of the performance and repeat those that she wishes to underline still further. Slight exaggeration can sometimes help in emphasising salient points.

After the model has been presented, the client should be asked to attempt to imitate the model. He should then be encouraged to rehearse the behaviour, with the counsellor giving him immediate feedback in the form of positive comments and suggestions about needed improvements. He should be reminded of the importance of such *behaviour rehearsal* in his own time.

The procedure for effective modelling may be summarised thus:

1 Ask the client to demonstrate how he typically acts.
2 Isolate effective and ineffective parts of his behaviour for observation, discussion, and practice.
3 Choose one or two of the ineffective behaviours and demonstrate a more effective way.
4 Repeat the demonstration several times if necessary, exaggerating the parts that cause difficulty.
5 Ask the client to rehearse the behaviour he has observed. Give him helpful feedback.
6 Continue rehearsing until a smooth, natural performance is achieved.
7 Repeat this process with other, more complex aspects of the client's behaviour.

When using modelling, it is important to begin with simple aspects of the client's behaviour. This helps to ensure that the client will experience success and improvement and will thus be willing and confident to attempt more complex behaviours. It is usually easier for clients to master simple non-verbal skills before attempting more complex verbal skills.

Part of a good modelling session might go something like this: 'Remember each point. You must always knock firmly. When he calls you in, stand up straight, push the door open, step into the room, look straight at him and smile. Got that? . . . Now before we go any further, you repeat those points to me . . . Good, now we'll both say them again, out loud, while you watch me do it. See, first I . . . then I . . . OK? Now, you try it while we both repeat the steps aloud once more . . . Very good. You did this, this, this, and this perfectly. But next time, up straighter and a bit firmer on the door knocking.'

EXERCISE 4.9

Plan modelling sessions with your partner, breaking up each of the following situations into two or three segments, each containing specific behaviours. Consider every detail – appearance, timing, gestures, posture, sequences, words, tone, facial expression. Then carry out each modelling segment, with your partner giving feedback on your performance.

(a) Entering an office to ask for a job.
(b) Facing a reputedly tough class for the first time.
(c) Making a complaint about a purchase.
(d) Rebuking someone who has jumped a queue.

Role-playing

Role-playing means acting out how a person with a particular title or function usually behaves. It is obviously akin to modelling and behaviour rehearsal, and all three are often used in conjunction with one another. But role-playing usually implies a less prescribed way of behaving. The emphasis is more upon feeling what it is like to act in a certain manner, sometimes with the further implication that the role, being different, is unfamiliar. The roles should not be played for long: three or four minutes is all that is necessary.

Some examples might help. A teacher plays a different role from a student, as does a nurse from a patient, and a counsellor or social worker from a client. If people pair off, play one of these roles and then switch to the other, ie, *reverse roles*, they might begin to experience what another person feels or thinks. As a result, those taking part would probably be better able to appreciate what actually goes on in such pairings. If they are professionals, such learning may help them to be more effective in their work.

The many opportunities for direct learning in role-playing and role reversal make them practical skills for counsellors to use in helping clients to change. These skills would be appropriate for a counsellor wishing to assist an adolescent boy who wanted to talk to his mother in a more adult fashion. She might first encourage him to try out several different ways of doing this while she played a parental role according to his instructions. He would thus be helped to experiment with alternatives within a safe setting. If both counsellor and client were then to reverse roles, the boy might thus, by acting out feelings and hunches, be able to anticipate more accurately how his mother might respond to the different approaches.

In both role-playing and role reversal the client should be encouraged, even coached, to throw himself into the parts he plays, with all the feelings, gestures, words, tones, and volume that are typically used, or that he wants to experiment with. The more convincingly the roles are enacted, the greater the number of learning opportunities and change possibilities that are offered to the client.

EXERCISE 4.10

Try short role-plays and role reversals for each of these situations:
(a) mother – daughter conflict
(b) worker – supervisor interview
(c) housewife – door-to-door salesman
(d) teacher – student conference about unsatisfactory work
(e) nurse – patient exchange about medicine not taken
(f) welfare agency receptionist – applicant for assistance
(g) minister – recently deserted wife

Using rewards
There is much current interest in finding out how to change people's behaviour in various settings (families, work places, schools, institutions) by systematically altering the associations between events or 'bits' of behaviour. The general name for this method of changing behaviour is *reinforcement*, which refers to the way in which one can increase or decrease the likelihood that certain events will occur. As a general rule, behaviour which is regularly and immediately followed by pleasant experiences tends to be repeated. Such behaviour is said to be rewarded or positively

reinforced. On the other hand, behaviour which is ignored or has unpleasant consequences becomes less likely to reappear.

In everyday life things often seem to be more complicated than that and to follow either different rules or no rules at all. This is partly because what is rewarding to one person in a particular setting may not be so to others in that setting or to the same person in a different setting. Generally, however, the apparent complexities and contradictions arise from the fact that we have not observed accurately enough what is in fact occurring. For example, the very threats and naggings that are intended to stop a child's misbehaviour at home or at school frequently have the opposite effect. In an apparently perverse way they serve to reinforce the unwanted behaviour. This is because misbehaviour is all that the adult has responded to, and the child gets little or no recognition or reward for good behaviour. Frequently in such a situation all desirable behaviour passes unnoticed and without commendation of any kind, and the only adult reaction (notice, even in the form of nagging) is to misbehaviour. The most effective way of dealing with a child who is misbehaving is by ignoring this if possible, and instead making pleasant comments about appropriate behaviour. This must be done immediately after it occurs, so that the desired behaviour is reinforced. Parents and teachers using such tactics for the first time are often startled at their effectiveness.

Counsellors should help clients to plan changes based on careful observation of exactly 'what is reinforcing what'. The combination of rewarding desired behaviour and ignoring inappropriate behaviour is especially powerful, although it may not be sufficient or appropriate in every case. It is nevertheless widely applicable; problems arising in groups, in family relationships, and in supervision or training situations can often be resolved by altering the reinforcements in this manner.

Most of the counselling techniques used in the beginning and developing stages include rewarding effects. Good eye-contact and other minimal encouragers are rewarding in that they help a client to feel accepted and induce him to keep talking. Topic-following and reflection of feeling have similar effects. Almost all techniques in the early stages reward intimacy, sharing, problem-exploration, and a search for solutions.

But there is another aspect of reward which the counsellor can use to get her client to focus on some matters rather than on others. A good counsellor uses her techniques selectively in a manner similar to that of the successful teacher or parent, reinforcing certain remarks and ignoring others. In this way she can effectively influence the course of a counselling session, for those client remarks to which she refers in any way (except a strongly disapproving one) tend to be enlarged upon, while those she ignores tend to be dropped. By talking about or showing interest in client remarks which refer to insights and plans for instance, the counsellor is rewarding problem-solving and positive attitudes. If at the same time the counsellor ignores or cuts off long complaints and harrowing tales (ie, does not reward them), she is discouraging irresponsibility, and is in effect saying, 'I don't want to hear any more war stories. Let's see what we can actually do about this problem.' (It is possible for the counsellor to ignore something that the client particularly wants to talk about. In a good relationship the effects of such a misjudgement can usually be overcome, for the client will raise the topic again if it is important to him.)

Simple counselling techniques with strong reward components are appropriate skills to teach to some clients. For example, a client lacking in conversational ability might be coached by the counsellor in basic attending skills. Used in social situations, these skills act as rewards to speakers who are thus encouraged to respond to the client by conversing with him. A client should be urged to practise such skills in his own time and to report on their effects. Responding skills would likewise be valuable as general social skills.

The counsellor should remember that reward techniques can operate in either direction, and that a client may use them on the counsellor, as well as vice versa.

Another useful reward technique involves getting the client to make a list of satisfying activities for himself, or for another person for whom he feels responsible. At first his list might include only the following: tending plants, chatting on the phone, walking the dog, listening to a record. His adolescent son or daughter might have a list like this: having a driving lesson, playing pool, going to a disco. In both instances at least a dozen items should be listed. The list can be regarded as a kind of menu from which many satisfying activities can be selected.

All these activities can then be used either as rewards to be enjoyed *after* a certain disliked task has been performed, or as substitutes – *instead of* some self-defeating behaviour. In the first instance the satisfaction of a coffee break or a driving lesson might be made to depend upon having done all chores or studied for two 40-minute periods. In the latter case a client may be urged to consult the list and choose an activity whenever he feels that he is becoming tense, or bored, or depressed. Thus, instead of sinking further into unpleasant thoughts and feelings, he might invite a friend to lunch or go out to the shop, and thus counter his depression or boredom.

EXERCISE 4.11

1 *Selective reinforcement*
Notice that each of the following client statements includes references to both feeling and an action that might be taken. Identify both parts of each statement, and then make up a simple reflection comment that reinforces the action part. For example:
Client: I get so annoyed! They just won't do what I tell them!
Counsellor: You would like them to co-operate with you more?
   (a) 'Actually I am pretty low just now. I wish I could get more work done.'
   (b) 'I can't seem to talk to my old man these days. He really makes me mad.'
   (c) 'My husband and I just don't do things together any more. Perhaps we're bored with each other.'
2 *Reinforcement menus*
Make a list of activities that might be satisfying to you if you were in each of these situations:

   (a) A young mother with two children under three years, living in a new suburb.
   (b) A 16-year-old apprentice mechanic, boarding away from home.
   (c) A woman recently widowed, no family, 45 years old.
   (d) A retired farmer living in a big city.

For each situation make a composite list from everyone's contributions.

5

Completing the problem-solving process

We now examine the skills involved in the fourth and fifth stages of the problem-solving sequence – implementing a strategy and evaluation.

THE SKILLS OF IMPLEMENTING STRATEGIES

Making records

Recording is a simple but very important skill because it provides one of the most powerful means of prompting behaviour change. The client who feels that she accomplishes little should be urged to keep a detailed diary of how she spends her day. The parent who complains about her child's misbehaviour or the teacher concerned about an unruly class should each be helped to organise a recording system showing what happens just before and just after each misbehaviour and also how often the misbehaviours occur.

Recording should be focused on one or two observable behaviours that are at the centre of the issue and that can be counted. Observations based on generalised behaviours and vague problems lead to useless records. It is impossible to get accurate information about things like inattentiveness, over-eating, disobedience, or poor communication without being precise about what these descriptions mean and how they are exemplified. Counsellors should help clients to clarify the problem by asking them specific questions: 'What exactly did you eat between each meal in each 24-hour period?' 'How many questions did you ask in that time?' 'How many times was she out of her seat during the lesson?'

Recording is hardly a counselling skill, but it is such a valuable aid to making good decisions about change that its importance must be stressed. Counsellors should urge clients to gather relevant information about their behaviour and the behaviour of others when considering behaviour change. In some instances keeping an impersonal, accurate record can induce change without the use of any other skills or methods.

Exercise 5.1

1 Choose a familiar TV advertisement and practise recording one behaviour, eg, How often is the name of the product or service presented? List all the adjectives used. How often does the model's head move? How many different camera shots are used?
2 Watch two people talking together. In different one-minute segments, record separate behaviours, one to each segment, eg, number of head movements, leg movements, arm movements. Compare your record with that of a partner.
3 Imagine that you are finding it difficult to fit everything into your day. Make a log of your activities yesterday from getting up to going to bed. Describe the activities in detail. Keep the log in at least half-hour segments. Explain to a partner in what respects this was a typical day, and in what respects it was unusual.

Bodily awareness, relaxation, activities
As part of the processes by which behaviour is changed, it can be very helpful for people to become more aware of and in control of their bodily sensations. Heightened awareness can help clients to identify their feelings more precisely. Take, for example, a client who says she feels childish when spoken to patronisingly.
'What do you mean, patronisingly?'
'Well, he says things like — "Typical woman, over-reacting again!"'
'So you feel childish. How do you react physically, then?'
'I get all churned up inside. I feel my face getting red, and I want to scream at him.'
Counsellors can make much use of such material, getting clients to 'tune into' and then act out bodily feelings as a way of reporting their typical behaviour.
Bodily awareness techniques can also be used to help clients to gain more control of themselves. Relaxation is an especially useful skill for this. Transcendental meditation, yoga, biofeedback,

and hypnosis are other examples of techniques with similar purposes. The advantages of relaxation are that it is easily taught and easily learned. In addition, relaxation can conveniently be used in a wide variety of real-life situations. It can also be useful as an adjunct to other counselling skills.

Relaxation is achieved by gradually loosening muscles in all parts of the body so that there is no tightness or tension anywhere. Full attention is required, so that different parts of the body are relaxed in sequence. It is possible to attain either complete relax- ation, so that the whole body is limp, or partial relaxation, which can be used as a way of coping with particular tensions, for example in the neck or stomach. Different degrees or levels of relaxation can be reached, from simply removing muscle tension to attaining a state of rest approximating sleep, sometimes in fact going to sleep.

A counsellor who senses that his client is very anxious while talking to him may help her to relax by getting her to do a few simple exercises. This may help her to face her problems more calmly in counselling.

'How about just leaning right back in the chair and taking three or four deep breaths . . . Slowly now, fill up your lungs . . . Slower yet, just relax your arms . . .'

She may be encouraged to relax in these ways in her ordinary life.

Relaxation can be used in preparing for some especially tense situation, such as an interview, examination, or important meeting. Counsellors should encourage clients to use partial relax- ation skills while actually in tense situations. It can also be a satisfying respite after a worrying or upsetting experience or physical exertion.

The following set of directions is typical of those used to attain a deep state of relaxation. Counsellors who often use relaxation methods usually have such directions readily available for clients in pamphlet form and recorded on cassette tapes, with the instruc- tions paced slowly enough to last about 20 minutes.

1 Lie flat on the back, placing the feet about 18 inches apart. The hands should rest lightly away from the trunk, with the palms up.
2 Close your eyes and gently move all the different parts of the body to create a general feeling of relaxation.
3 Then start relaxing the body part by part. First think of the right leg. Inhale and slowly raise the leg about one foot off the floor. Hold it fully tensed. After five seconds, exhale abruptly and

relax the muscles of the right leg, allowing it to fall to the floor on its own. Shake the leg gently from right to left, relax it fully, and forget about the existence of this leg.

4 Repeat this same process with the left leg, and then with both hands, one at a time.

5 Then bring the mind to the muscles of the pelvis, buttocks, and anus. Tense them and relax. Once again, tense them and relax. Next, think of the abdomen. Inhale deeply through the nose and bloat the abdomen. Hold your breath for five seconds and suddenly let the air out through the mouth, simultaneously relaxing all the muscles of the abdomen and diaphragm.

6 Move up to the chest region. Inhale deeply through the nose, bloating the chest. Hold your breath for five seconds and suddenly let the air burst out through the mouth while relaxing all the muscles of the chest and diaphragm.

7 Move on to the shoulders. Without moving the forearms off the floor, try to make the shoulders meet in front of the body. Then relax and let them drop to the floor.

8 Slowly, gently, turn the neck right and left, right and left, then back to centre, mentally relaxing the neck muscles.

9 Coming to the facial muscles, move the jaw up and down, left and right a few times, then relax. Squeeze the lips together in a pout, then relax. Suck in the cheek muscles, then relax. Tense the tip of the nose, then relax. Wrinkle the forehead muscles, then relax.

10 Now you have relaxed all the muscles of the body. To make sure of this, allow your mind to wander over you entire body from the tips of the toes to the head, searching for any spots of tension. If you come across any spots of tension, concentrate upon this part and it will relax. If you do this mentally, without moving any muscle, you will notice that the part concerned obeys your command.

This is complete relaxation. Even your mind is at rest now. You may keep watching your breath, which will keep flowing in and out quite freely and calmly. Observe your thoughts without trying to take your mind anywhere. You are a witness, not a body or a mind but an ocean of peace and tranquillity. Remain in this condition at least five minutes. Do not become anxious about anything. When you decide to wake from this conscious sleep, do so quite slowly. Imagine that fresh energy is gently entering each part of your body, from the head down to the toes. Then slowly sit up. This exercise helps create a refreshed and peaceful feeling for the body and mind. Try to do this one to three times a day, especially upon rising and before retiring.

[*These directions for relaxation are reprinted by permission of* PREVENTION. *Copyright 1977, Rodale Press Inc. Emmaus, Pennyslvania. All rights reserved.*]

The reduction of tension by taking up some physical activity should also be recognised as a useful way of helping clients to change their behaviour. A game that demands some exertion of energy and permits some social interaction reduces tension and can serve as an excellent reward. However, solitary active pursuits may be preferred by some. Physical activities can reduce the many stresses that come from modern living – mentally and emotionally demanding experiences and boring, solitary, and sedentary occupations. Similar functions can be served by many other pursuits such as dancing, hobbies, games, arts and crafts, and playing and listening to music. It would be wise to encourage clients to include in every 'reinforcement menu' some physical or creative activity.

EXERCISE 5.2

In pairs or in a small group practice the 10 steps to relaxation described above. Discuss the experience, and list possible uses you may find for relaxation.

Thoughts and imagery

A counsellor's ability to deal directly and constructively with his client's mental activity is another important counselling skill. The client's thoughts, ideas, and perceptions are obviously important throughout counselling, so much so that their uses in changing behaviour are often overlooked. A good example of how imagery can be used is shown by the ways in which relaxation is taught. Besides the usual method of directing his client to relax various muscle groups, the counsellor may encourage her to recall or imagine events and situations which help the physical processes. This imagery encourages the loosening of her muscle tension. Physical tightness in her body may be reduced if she can call up images associated with calm, comfort, and rest. The counsellor prompts her to do this by using colourful language and a suitable tone of voice:

'Imagine you are on soft cushions in a dimly lit room with quiet slow music.'

'Notice how slow, and deep, and easy your breathing is now.'

'Feel all the tightness easing away as though you were in a warm bath.'

At various points in a counselling relationship, thinking and imagination can be profitably used to help the change process. For example, the counsellor should encourage his client to use similar sorts of descriptions and language to fill out what she means by such general terms as 'a real scene', 'not so good', 'feeling better'. He should try to get her to think, imagine, and describe things in concrete and colourful detail in response to such questions and requests as these:

1 'Tell me how you're feeling right now, when you're saying that you feel trapped. What does your body seem to be saying to you?'
2 What does he do then? How do you think he feels at those moments? And how do you feel when he says and does those things?'

Some clients seem to have too active an imagination, and most of their difficulties seem to arise from the way they concentrate on negative aspects of their thoughts. These people become more and more anxious and resistant to change because they constantly anticipate failure, and as a result they avoid facing up to things. In whatever ways he can, the counsellor should stop the clients from dwelling on these aspects. He can reinforce talk about alternatives, he can ignore references to negative aspects, and he can point out in a rational manner the self-defeating nature of such thoughts. He can also elicit from his client 'reinforcement menus' of images which have pleasant associations, and to which she can be urged to turn whenever negative images intrude. Such a programme of 'guided fantasy' would of course need to be supported and supplanted as soon as possible by more active steps to bring the images into reality.

A rather dramatic technique called *thought-stopping* is a further example of the use that some counsellors make of the clients' mental activities in trying to change their behaviour. It is sometimes used to help clients who constantly engage in unproductive talk. If, for example, the client begins expressing her doubts or fears for the tenth time, the counsellor might interrupt her. He might say firmly, 'Stop that, right now!' and emphasise his point with a gross movement such as thumping his chair, or standing up, or turning away. By this means he might succeed in directing her to talk about something else that could lead to constructive action.

Obviously the success of such a technique depends upon a sound counsellor-client relationship and upon good judgement by the counsellor. An extension of this technique is sometimes useful. If the counsellor should find that certain situations seem to prompt negative thoughts in the client, he might encourage her to devise a thought-stopping signal for herself. It might be in the form of a note in a conspicuous place that says, 'Stop complaining!' or 'Don't apologise!'

EXERCISE 5.3

As counsellor, plan how you would encourage a client (your partner) to think positively, and in concrete detail about:
(a) Cooking a special evening meal for the family.
(b) Going to bed in a relaxed way.
(c) Getting ready for work on a Monday.
(d) Having a relative to stay for a week when it does not really suit.

Desensitisation
This approach to changing behaviour uses several techniques together, including thinking, relaxing, and imagining. In effect the counsellor tries to inoculate the client against fears and anxieties that have become very intense in a particular situation. He does this by using the client's relaxed bodily state to counter the tensed bodily sensations that arise when she recalls situations in which she was frightened or anxious. There are several considerations and distinct stages in the process.

1 The technique is most appropriately used with clients who are anxious about only one specific matter, eg, examination fears, a dread about aircraft, or fear of blood.
2 Before beginning, the process should be fully explained to the client and her feelings about it explored. Unless she accepts that change is possible and that most fears are learnt and can be unlearnt, the process will not work.
3 First the client must learn to relax deeply when instructed or at will.
4 The next step is for the counsellor and client together to work out a list of the events that are associated with the fear. These are then sorted into a series (or hierarchy) from least feared to most feared. The least feared are usually those most remote in time and place from the situation of major concern.
   A hierarchy of examination fear might begin with 'thinking about the exam three weeks beforehand', and end with 'sitting

in the exam room picking up the paper'. Since the hierarchy is important, the counsellor should try to elicit at least 10 items from the client. It can be useful to try sorting them on to a scale, assigning a value of 0 to the least and 100 to the very worst, and filling in as many of the intermediate values as possible. The thinking and imagining involved in this stage are very important parts of the process.

5 In the next stage the counsellor first helps the client to achieve a state of deep physical relaxation by adding as much mentally relaxing imagery as possible. Then he describes the lowest item in the fear hierarchy to her. If she signals that it is distressing to imagine that item (eg, by raising a finger), he helps her to relax and concentrate on other pleasant images until she feels able to cope. Not giving a signal means that she can tolerate that item. He then introduces the next item.

6 In this way the two of them gradually work up the hierarchy. The counsellor urges the client to practise the essentials of the technique in her own time, and to do whatever she can to support herself in the real situation when the anxiety occurs (eg, deep breathing, partial relaxation, thought-stopping).

EXERCISE 5.4

In counsellor-client pairs, the client talks about (a) a pleasant, exciting experience, and (b) an extremely unpleasant experience. As counsellor, help the client to describe the details of each experience as vividly as possible. Try to arrange the details of each experience into a hierarchy from least pleasant (unpleasant) to most pleasant. Try to spread the items on a scale from 0 to 100.

Mixing strategies

Desensitisation is a notable example of a technique which involves several different counselling skills in combination. Once the various separate skills of counselling and change processes have been mastered, counsellors are urged to combine them as they see fit. Many combinations are possible, and books on counselling often describe these as mixed or multiple strategies.

Skills developed by gestalt counsellors exemplify such approaches well by combining imagery, bodily awareness, and role-playing. Assertion training schemes likewise show how counsellors can help people by using a mixture of strategies. Typically such training involves the use of rational planning, imagery, modelling, and role-playing, followed by careful rehearsal of actions, words, and feelings. The result is that people who usually are not able to say what they want to because of being either too timid or too domineering, learn to express themselves more effectively.

REVIEW EXERCISE 5.5*

1 Using a verbatim transcript of a counselling interview, identify the skills used in every counsellor lead. Compare your answers with those of others. This exercise will help you to review many of the skills discussed in the previous three chapters and will indicate those about which there is still some uncertainty.
2 With the client's permission, record a counselling interview using an audio recorder. Analyse the interview as follows:
   (a) Transcribe verbatim two sets of 15 consecutive interactions from any two sections of the interview.
   (b) Critically analyse the transcribed portions of the interview by identifying the skill used, its intended effect and its actual effect. In addition, look for patterns of skill usage, indications of a typical style, and any inappropriate leads or assumptions that influence the course of the interview.
   This exercise can be repeated over time. It can serve as a check on one's progress, proficiency, and effectiveness. See the example on page 157.
3 Make a brief video or audio programme illustrating the effective use of a skill or skills. This is an excellent way of demonstrating a working understanding of particular counselling skills.

Homework
Once clients have expressed their goals in specific terms, homework can be planned to accomplish those goals. This is a way of ensuring that the process of change continues outside the counselling session and gives clients the opportunity to practise new behaviours and learn new skills. Ideally the homework would be decided on jointly, following discussion about its purpose and likely outcome. To be effective homework should be:
(a) clearly stated (what to do, when to do it, where to do it and in what amount it should be done);
(b) manageable and relevant to the client's problem;
(c) designed to ensure success. Accomplishing small tasks can build up the client's self-confidence and lead to greater successes.

At the next counselling session the homework should be reviewed.

EXERCISE 5.6

1 First, state a specific goal for each of the general goals listed below. Then write a homework assignment that might lead to each of these goals:
(a) losing weight; (b) improving my appearance; (c) standing up to my mother; (d) getting fit; (e) not boring other people; (f) controlling the class better; (g) getting on top of the job; (h) taking a break. For each goal list the behaviours suggested by the group.

THE SKILLS OF EVALUATION

Assessing results
As soon as possible after the client has carried out a behaviour change plan, the counsellor should discuss the experience with her. The factors that contributed to success should be identified so that she will be encouraged to try again. The sequence of events leading up to the episode and the details of the episode itself should be recounted. The counsellor should also discuss with the client how she felt, and remind her of the satisfactions she achieved. She should be encouraged to re-experience those pleasant feelings as vividly as possible, as these will act as inducements for her to repeat her first success.

The value of repetition and practice should be stressed and the client should be urged to repeat the task as often as necessary. If she is hesitant, the counsellor should remind her of the 'pay-offs' she is getting for her performance.

EXERCISE 5.7

In pairs, one person tells of an actual or imagined experience in which the outcome was successful, but about which there had been considerable uncertainty and anxiety beforehand. Begin with an example from the previous exercise. The other person asks questions that bring out reasons for the success. Then reverse the roles.

Summarising
Summarising is the process of tying together all that has been communicated during part or all of the counselling session. It attempts to bring together the main highlights of what has occurred thereby clarifying what has been accomplished and what remains to be done. Summarising also serves as a natural means of finishing a session or beginning a new one.

It is often effective to have the client summarise what has happened or been discussed. This enables the counsellor to get a better understanding of the client's view of things and helps the client see what progress has been made.

When summarising, the counsellor should try to pull together the most salient points, state them as simply and clearly as possible and ask the client for her reaction to the accuracy of the summary.

For example:

Counsellor: Let's see if we can put all of this together. On the one hand you feel lonely and isolated, especially with groups of people. On the other hand, you say that you find it hard to mix with others even on a one-to-one basis. So, even though you want to get to know others, there is no easy way to begin. Is that it?

EXERCISE 5.8

Discuss a topic with a partner. The topic should be something of concern or interest to both people. Note that this need not be a role-play situation in which one person is designated counsellor and the other client.

Every few minutes ask someone (the leader, trainer, or a person designated as timekeeper) to interrupt and ask that each person attempt to summarise what has happened to that point. Before allowing discussion to continue, make sure each person agrees that his partner's summary is accurate.

EXERCISE 5.9

Notice how often the interviewer in a radio or television news or current affairs panel discussion uses the skill of summarising.

Generalising

Generalising is the skill of pointing out to clients that they can follow the process used in counselling and apply the same communication skills in other aspects of their lives in the future.

For example, the problem-solving approach followed during counselling could be made explicit to the client with the suggestion that it could be used in the future.

'You may have noticed the process we've been going through during our counselling sessions. First of all we identified your problem and then set some goals. Later we worked out how to reach these goals and then discussed how well this had been achieved. You might like to go through a similar process when you have other decisions to make or problems to overcome in the future.'

Likewise a family which has been taught to use 'I' messages could be reminded to continue to use them, especially during disputes.

'Remember how I've encouraged you to use "I" messages to express feelings during our meetings. For example, "I feel hurt when you don't thank me for cooking the tea because it seems I'm taken for granted." Now that we're finishing our sessions I'd just like to point out that it would be helpful if you carried on communicating in that way.'

One way of emphasising that the skills and process of communication during counselling are generalisable is to provide written material that clients can take away with them as a reminder.

Referral

If the counsellor decides that his client has needs that he cannot meet, he should consider referring her to another agency or individual. Assuming that he has first appraised his client's needs carefully, he should adopt the following principles and procedures.

1 The counsellor should first find out whether another agency provides the necessary services. This requires a thorough knowledge of community resources for helping (eg, employment, residential care, medical, recreational, rehabilitative, educational), including their policies, programmes, costs, and limitations. It is also important to know agencies' rules and all relevant statutory obligations.
2 Having selected an appropriate agency, the counsellor should then discuss the case with the person in the agency who would probably receive the referral, taking care, however, not to disclose confidential information about his client.
3 If a referral seems appropriate, it should then be discussed with the client. The counsellor should prepare her for it, explaining honestly and clearly his decision to refer her to that particular agency. He should encourage her to react to the proposal and, if possible, to participate in the actual decision. He should also take into account the possibility that she may think that her problem is insoluble if he cannot help her further.
4 When a referral has been agreed upon, definite arrangements should be made so that the client knows exactly when and where to go and whom to ask for. In some cases the counsellor might decide to accompany the client on the first occasion.

5 The counsellor should take care to provide the agency with relevant information about the client, including:
   (a) a clear statement of her problem or needs;
   (b) a summary of the help that has been given;
   (c) a request for a specific service for her;
   (d) an indication of her feelings about referral.
6 After the referral has been completed, the counsellor should be prepared to co-operate in some way if asked to do so by the referral agency. Whether he continues to be actively involved in the case or not, he should seek a progress report from the agency so that he can assess the usefulness of the referral.

In all decisions regarding referral, the counsellor should be guided by his estimate of his client's best interests. In dealing with her, he should continue to be open, honest, and supportive, and he should act only with her consent.

Termination
Termination may occur at any time – most obviously when the objectives of the counselling relationship have been reached. It may also result from an agreement at the outset that only one topic or problem would be dealt with, or that there would be a specified number of sessions.

Besides estimating the client's readiness to cope alone, the counsellor should be aware of his own reactions. It is understandable that a counsellor would regret losing contact with a client who, for instance, had been pleasant to work with, had made much progress, and had openly expressed her gratitude. Again, however, the relevant criterion is the client's best interests: sooner or later this means her independence from the counsellor.

The termination phase should begin with the counsellor, and whenever possible the client, reviewing and summarising what has happened in counselling. There could be reference to both the original goals and the results, and also to the time that has elapsed. An appropriate note to end on could be the counsellor's preparedness to continue on a 'call-me-if-you-need-me' basis, coupled with his indicating that he expected not to be contacted because he had faith in her ability to cope.

SUMMARY EXERCISE

Exercise 5.10 provides an opportunity to practise the first four steps of the problem-solving sequence in one interview. As a reminder, these steps are repeated here, with examples of typical counsellor tasks. Note that in a real situation the counsellor and client would still need to evaluate results at a later date.

1 The initial aim is to identify the problem, ie, to change general problems into specific, behaviour-related problems.
Counsellor's tasks
(a) Clarify the meaning of general words or phrases.
   'Tell me what you mean when you say . . .'
(b) Ask for specific examples and descriptions of circumstances.
   'Tell me of a specific instance . . .'

2 The next step is to set goals, ie, what would the client prefer to happen?
Counsellor's tasks
(a) How would the client rather act?
   'Tell me what you would rather . . .'
(b) What could the client do to overcome the problem?
   'How do you think you could handle . . .'

3 The client should be encouraged to work out how to achieve those goals and to explore the implications and consequences of each one.
Counsellor's tasks
(a) Help the client make a realistic choice, ie, consider physical, emotional, and social factors.
   'How are you going to choose . . .'
   'Which seems the best and why?'
(b) Help the client to understand advantages and disadvantages of each alternative.
   'What do you see as the advantages (disadvantages) of . . .'

4 Finally, the client should try to identify the changes or new skills that she needs to accomplish the chosen strategy.
Counsellor's tasks
(a) Help the client identify deficiencies.
   'What will you have to do/learn/buy etc . . .?'
(b) Help the client take steps to overcome deficiencies.
   'Let's start by trying . . .'

EXERCISE 5.10

1 Divide into pairs and decide who will play the role of counsellor and who will play the client. Using one of the role-play situations described below, the counsellor leads the client

through the problem-solving sequence described above. The counsellor should move from one stage to the next only when the first step has been satisfactorily covered.

2 When finished, the participants should swap roles and repeat the role-play situation below.

3 When both persons have played counsellor, discuss the usefulness of the problem-solving sequence in the larger group setting. For example, people may want to comment on how easy the sequence was to follow, how useful it was as a guide or indicator of progress, or its relevance to a real counselling situation.

Role-play 1: The client begins by saying he would like to be more at ease in groups.

Role-play 2: The client says that his children are able to manipulate him too easily.

6

Nga matapihi o te waiora (Windows on Māori well-being)

When woven together, the human threads are strong ropes which pull together in times of stress and need.

Counselling as a one-to-one relationship between a professional and a client is a concept foreign to Māori culture. In Māoridom, helping involves the whole whānau (family) and beyond in an intense sharing which takes physical, emotional, spiritual, and practical forms. The essential elements are the family network (whanaungatanga), the help given by the people (manaakitanga), and the spiritual dimension (wairuatanga).

I wish to open windows on to my personal experience of these elements of Māoritanga (what it means to be a Māori), which shows how help is given within our culture. I do not intend to suggest a set of counselling activities or skills that readers might find useful in helping Māori to solve their problems. Instead I wish to broaden your vision with my lifetime of perceiving, to plumb the depths of your emotion with my experience, to use simple but descriptive language to paint scenarios so that you may see, feel, and know the kinds of situations met and resolved. It is not easy to express or explain how a small area of living can be divorced from the whole life-style of a people. Because Māori people think laterally, I must ask the reader to have an open mind and see not only what is written but to also look beyond to the whole of living.

Many cultures have intruded into the Māori life-style but never for long enough to break the strong humanistic and spiritual fibres which are uniquely interwoven into Māoritanga, or as John Rangihau (a well-known elder of the Tuhoe tribe) once stated, 'Tuhoetanga', or in my case, 'Maniapototanga' – where my tribal roots are. Culture is a life-style experienced, supported, and perpetuated by the community in which a person lives. It constantly evolves, changing according to the values and demands made by the community. Māoritanga is a deep-rooted culture, but it must be realised that tribal areas have their own individual culture, even though there is a strong bond of similarity in many aspects of tribal living. As with the diversity of dialects, so too is there a diversity of cultural practices among tribes. The Māori people do not see this diversity as a dilemma, but view it as a richness in the way each tribe may direct its own development for the betterment of its community.

There are many different cultures throughout the world, within one's own country, and even in one's own home town. So it should not be surprising that Māoritanga has many cultures. There is the Māori in the cities and the country, in educational centres and at lower levels of economic affluence. The same is true of Pākehātanga (non-Māori culture). However, each group will tend to view culture only from its own perspective, either with blinkers or with a wider vision. The level of understanding will be limited to the boundaries each group or each individual sets. Thus, I just look inwardly so that I can begin to write what it means to see through my eyes, feel through my own emotional experiences, and say with my own mixture of Māori and English vocabulary what counselling is in Maniapototanga, the tribal area within which I live and work. From what I have written the reader may then be better able to understand and help Māori people resolve some of the problems that beset them.

For generations now there has been a slow deterioration of health, and social and spiritual well-being among the Māori. The degradation of the people is constantly portrayed from a European perspective: the scenes of drug-related violence, the alcohol-based family dysfunction, and the apparently apathetic attitudes of many towards employment. Economic measures initiated by governments have not assisted the people. If anything, they have left the people dependent and quite helpless with the kind of piecemeal security that has been offered. Both Māori and Pākehā have undergone the same treatment, but each group has dealt with the situation differently. Most Pākehā families have become even more nuclear, a situation to which they have long been accustomed. As individuals they can more easily think about their own future and move comfortably away to make a life of their own without family support. The Māori, however, has had a lifetime of tribal thinking, of tribal support, of tribal co-operation.

As stated previously, culture is deep-rooted and difficult to change. When a people accustomed to lateral thinking and working co-operatively is isolated, and its families are asked to become nuclear, divorced from their tribes, many problems begin to appear. Disharmony arises within the nuclear family as well as within the tribal grouping. Among Māori, self-realisation is frowned upon as something you don't do. The tribal group has always selected the chosen families or individuals for further teaching, or to take the progressive steps forward, with the knowledge that the benefits gained by that family or individual will be available to the tribe or families. By way of analogy, when we look at the forest we see the different kinds of trees vying for supremacy and recognition. But always within that forest there are the low-lying shrubs which support and shade the 'feet' of the giants that grow tall and proud. So, too, must the tribe look after its own 'giants'. They must shade the feet of their kaumātua (elders), or the chosen few who would be unable to stand tall without family and tribal support.

The kaumātua are usually carefully selected according to rigid guidelines set many years ago by tribal members who had a great deal of knowledge and mana (power). Therefore, whanaungatanga plays an important part in the progress or apathy of the tribal members. A well chosen leader, or kaumātua, is one who knows how to encourage the best from people, a person who can stand back and allow development to progress with a gentle prod when the need arises.

Whānau means family, whanaunga means a relative, and whanaungatanga means the relatedness of people, one with another. When the deeper meaning of the network in whanaungatanga is explored, it becomes clear how the Māori allocated responsibilities for the children. The eldest child, mātāmua, is designated to be the repository of family history. Hence the reason for the first born being 'adopted' by the grandparents who proceed to patiently sing, recite, or tell very important family history and/or issues which one day will become pivotal issues for action. Just as every tree has a place in the forest, every member of the whānau has a responsibility within the whānau structure. The mātāmua and the pōtiki (youngest) have the more important responsibilities of leadership, repositories of knowledge, singers/composers of songs, and keepers of the land and family taonga (heirlooms) which have been inherited.

To illustrate how whanaungatanga can be such a strong bond within the family or tribe I would like to describe my mother's illness and death. My mother had nine children by her first husband, some of whom she lost in childbirth or during the influenza epidemic years. I remember only four of the children: the eldest son (mātāmua), who had been brought up by my mother's parents; the youngest son (pōtiki) who sought and acquired his own knowledge of things Māori by associating with the kaumātua of many marae; and two daughters, one of whom died of consumption in my lap when I was four years of age. We children knew of death and childbirth as part of everyday living and coped well with the aid of the extended family's support.

I was one of the five children from my mother's second marriage. I remember, however, many children from the extended family living with us in my early days of youth. If there had ever been a roll call for all the children she fostered, fed, and finally sent on their way, about twenty to thirty people would be listed. Even grown men and women came to live with us for up to two to three years. My father accepted the role of breadwinner, entertainer, and 'co-counsellor' during all these times without question. Throughout her life my mother gave freely of herself.

When she became very ill with cancer at the age of 92, she was never without company to relieve the boredom of lying in pain with which she coped so easily. The news of her many fostered children helped her forget her pain. Her children came to her side to support her and she sent them away laughing and joking about the anecdotes of life she would relate to them. My daughter had given up her nursing job to be there at home or in the hospitals, wherever my mother was being treated for her cancer. It was she who saw the strength of the human bonds which her grandmother had woven as a mother. In the year that she was ill and confined to bed, whanaungatanga came to feed her, to wash her, to talk and play cards with her, to sing to her, and to pray with her.

When death came her tangi (the time of grieving) was three days of continuous streams of people coming to pay their last respects to a woman they loved and respected. No verbal expressions of sympathy were needed. Instead, the sharing of love, tears, and tasks were given to support the bereaved family who kept watch by her side. Throughout her life my mother had taught us humility, manaakitanga, and a deep sense of spirituality. There were over 1500 people at her funeral with both Māori and Pākehā bowed in respect and quiet grief. Many were children she had succoured and many were mothers of the children she had helped to deliver. All had been touched by this woman who had supported them in their time of need. Even today my filial bond with her gives me a sense of humility as well as admiration for someone who had the gift of loving all fellow people. Both young and old came to cry with me for someone we all respected and loved deeply. In this story we see not only blood ties but the social ties which bind people together for a common cause.

Each of the whānau members had a part to play in the rituals of sharing grief. My role was to receive the visiting whanaunga who came to grieve with us, to support us, and to share the workload of feeding the large groups of people who had come from far and wide. My brothers saw to the needs of the people: meals, beds, and cups of tea with every new group's arrival. My own children saw to the needs of the support group who stayed in the wharemate to keep me and my family company. My major responsibility was to take care of my father — he had lost a helpmate of nearly sixty years. Her passing left a huge gap that no one could fill because of the tremendous mana she had held within the family and Ngati Maniapoto. For the ten years before her illness she had helped others in their times of grief and so they too came to help my father in his grief. When woven together, the human threads are strong ropes which pull together in times of stress and need. These taura tangata (the humanistic fibres) were formed by the years of weaving together of people who had been touched by my mother.

This is only one example of whanaungatanga and manaakitanga. Recently at John Rangihau's tangi this physical expression of respect and sympathy was also present, not for one day but for the length of time that the body lay in state. I have yet to feel the same support and see the same kind of pooling of strengths to help the bereaved Pākehā family. Early criticisms of these Māori rituals showed the low level of importance that Pākehā people attached to the time of grieving. Support for the bereaved Māori family is given by extended family and friends alike. It begins when the need arises and continues for many months afterwards, culminating when the bereaved family hold the huritau, the commemoration service where thanks are given to the extended family for their continued support throughout the time of grieving. Invitations to the huritau are sent out by word of mouth and the 'grapevine's' value is shown by the number of people who attend.

Another window I would like to open shows how a part of my family coped with a stress situation that was fraught with a diversity of problems.

Because of their inability to have children of their own, Mr and Mrs R had adopted three children, two boys and a girl. The children were closely related to their adopted mother, so the whanaungatanga bonds were strong. The eldest, a son, was married with six children ranging from three to eleven years. Two of his children lived permanently with Mr and Mrs R but both knew their natural parents and moved comfortably between the two couples. The other four children preferred to stay with their grandparents but liked to be with parents as well.

The daughter was well educated, loved by many people and highly respected by her employers who appreciated her initiative, confidence, and dedication. She worked in a laundromat and assisted the local chemist in balancing his ledgers. Throughout her working time of four or five years she had not saved her money, although her income was considerable, but instead spent much of it on nieces, nephews, and her parents. The youngest son and his girlfriend had a child who has born prematurely and lived the first six months or so in an oxygen tent at the hospital and later at home with his grandparents. Even after the need for the oxygen tent had passed, the child was frequently hospitalised because of his delicate condition.

At the beginning of the financial year both Mr R and his eldest son were put off work and given severance pay. The younger son began to seek his own accommodation, but still had the responsibility of an ailing child and the stress of having only short-term employment. While this was going on, the R's daughter had a mild attack of influenza. While she was at home with her parents sick, her elder brother decided his marriage was over and walked out. His wife brought all of their six children to their grandparents, along with all the woes of her household. Next, the younger son's child became alarmingly sick. After a week in bed the 'flu-stricken daughter complained constantly of a headache which the family doctor could not suppress with the drugs he administered. Eventually she was hospitalised and operated on to relieve the pressure caused by her brain swelling. From then on she was in a deep coma. Thus, in a very short span of time the family was faced with an only daughter in a deep coma, a very sick and helpless baby with young parents, the eldest son's marriage breakdown with attendant family upheavals, and a caring husband and wife who did not know which way to turn.

What happened during those months was a nightmare that Mr and Mrs R will never forget. But, as illustrated in the previous example of whanaungatanga support at a tangi, so in this case the whanaungatanga lightened their stress load. The six weeks that the daughter spent in intensive care was not spent in total isolation with medical attendants alone caring for her. She was constantly massaged, talked and sung to, and attended to by the immediate family while the extended family tended to the other problems. All the grandchildren came home to grandad who monitored their school attendance and other daily chores. Extended family members took care of the washing and meal preparation to free grandmother who sat and attended to her daughter daily.

Eventually the daughter was taken off the life support machines. The care given by medical attendants and family began to revive her muscular movements and she began to respond to the singing and constant chatter of her nieces and nephews. The first time she moved her fingers marked a real breakthrough. The pay-off for continued medical treatment and physical attention came when the daughter walked out of the hospital after three months. She continued to improve and was soon able to continue her life as though nothing had happened.

There were improvements in other areas of the family as well. The elder brother returned home to settle the children in with the grandparents; he learned to shoulder his own responsibilities and understood that the children needed a more stable environment. His wife secured employment and pursued her own self-development. Both realised there was no coming together again, but the children were again able to move comfortably between parents and grandparents.

The hapless child finally died two months later, but both parents were supported by the extended family throughout their ordeal. During his sister's ordeal the youngest son too was a constant hospital visitor. He spent as much of his time with his sister as he did with his child in the children's intensive care unit. At the child's tangi, held at the grandparent's home, the support was physically noticeable. It was there that Mr R spoke, saying that he, his wife, and family were deeply grateful for the support that was given when they needed it most. Manaakitanga (assistance) came from many quarters: from relations, friends, bosses, schools, and even the shopkeepers for whom his daughter had worked.

Among Māori, whanaungatanga support is an inbuilt method of assisting people in stressful situations. In the situation with Mr and Mrs R it was apparent that the most important issue was the health of their daughter who had given so much of her own life, savings, and time to help them with their children. The other matters became the responsibility of others in the whānau. Both sons were supported by their father but in return they needed to support their mother who had the major task of reviving their sister.

I was not the only family member to assist them but the bond with them was so strong that I travelled to the hospital at least once a week to reassure my brother. The knowledge that someone else was there to talk to, to massage their daughter and to give them spiritual sustenance was a comfort to them. There were many of us who filled that role and did it without question. Nothing is more disheartening than a continual bombardment of situations which tests one's ability to cope. We knew this and we wanted to give them the assurance of our care. In times of stress the physical presence of a person, especially a family member, gives that assurance, so we travelled to the hospital to answer the call of whanaungatanga.

For those who are not spiritually moved, wairuatanga (spirituality) can be a difficult concept to understand, but I will try to describe, in my own way, how it is with me. I believe that everyone has a spirit, a soul, a wairua. Each wairua has mana according to a person's status or strength of character. One's wairua can be severely damaged during times of stress, and the physical presence of one's family can be very nurturing. Whenever one is alone one can conjure up the spirits of one's ancestors to seek solace and assurance. There have been times when the mere mention of my mother's name has given me the reassurance I needed to carry on. Her mana is so strong that I almost feel the physical presence of her being. During my brother's troublesome times my father, who is my medium, gave us very reassuring words of wisdom. Each time he did this I felt as though my mother was speaking because the words and the manner in which they were given were identical to hers. So, physical and spiritual assurance can span the miles and years when there is togetherness.

But spirituality is more than that to me. I feel it most when there is a pōwhiri (welcome ceremony) on a marae. It does not matter whether the ceremony is small or large, the feeling that others are there, in addition to those physically present, is very strong. When I hear the calls of the kaikaranga expressing feelings of sadness or joy, my thoughts span the distance of time to the elders who first expressed those feelings to me in my youth. I view the visitors and see, too, the images of those ancestors; I listen and I hear their voices; and I bow in respect for those who earlier trod the hills and paved the way for us who follow.

One day when I was at a marae (tribal meeting place), I was asked to give a lecture to about forty adult students. Not having prepared anything, I was shocked, honoured, and saddened, all at the same time. I had seen a cemetery close by so I turned to those buried there for inspiration. I shall never forget that lecture there – I astounded myself with a flow of ideas which continued for one and a half hours. Someone later asked me for my lecture notes, but I had none to give. Before I left that marae, I stood and thanked those buried there for the wonderful visions that they had given me so I could share my beliefs and thoughts with those students. Today I still ask my deceased elders to support me and will continue to do so. Perhaps it is a quiet moment of reflection that brings memories of people in one's life.

In pre-European times when children were born, each one was designated a task and they were sung to by their parents.

Girls born to the tribe were given different tasks like weaving, singing, reciting genealogy, or caring for people. All these concepts were sung to them, and their hands strengthened by massaging to make them pliant and strong for weaving. By the time they were older they had acquired the basics for the tasks ahead. If the child was a boy and the family wanted to set a task of revenge for a slight meted out by another family, the story of the whole incident would be sung and the son would be prepared for the task ahead of him. In later years he would remember the songs and would undertake the task of either revenge or reconciliation depending on the options given by the composers of the song. Was this a form of conditioning? Perhaps, but it worked to ensure that children carried out the wishes of their parents.

There are many waiata (songs) written in Pei Te Hurinui Jones's *Nga Moteatea* that illustrate this theme. Three years ago I was reminded quietly by my father of the prophetic words of my uncle, who had a strong influence on my life. His voice still resounds in my mind when I recall the past. I have him to thank for the directions I have taken. Although they are long dead, my uncle and mother are my spiritual guardians. I feel them, I talk to them, and at times there are physical visions to redirect or assure me.

The windows I have opened are personal experiences, but behind each one there are counselling messages. The main threads are: 1) *Whanaungatanga* (family networks); 2) *Manaakitanga* (assistance given by people); 3) *Wairuatanga* (spiritual support). Intertwined with these is the 'aroha' that pervades all of them, the binding agent and the most important ingredient in counselling. Aroha has many meanings: loving, caring, supporting, saddening, but aroha is certainly an emotive word. Aroha is a name, an idea for a composition, a theme for a song (as the song says, 'Love is a Many Splendoured Thing'). The windows are yours to look through. If you see what I have tried to paint, you will recognise these feelings. If the vision is clouded and your emotions have not been stirred, then you are meant to read more. There are many able authors who have painted amazing pictures: Witi Ihimaera in *Tangi*; Patricia Grace in *Potiki*; Keri Hulme in *The Bone People*. The poetry of Hone Tuwhare contains exquisite cameos of human relationships. Several useful books, including the ones mentioned here, are listed in the select bibliography at the end of this book. My hope is that the illustrations I have provided have been useful in portraying the supportive networks used in Maori counselling.

Arohanui,

Hinekahukura Barrett-Aranui*

*Hinekahukura Barrett-Aranui, a member of the Ngati-Uekaha hapū of the Maniopoto tribe, is a counsellor and Māori language teacher at Piopio College in the King Country, North Island.

7

Family counselling

In this book counselling skills have been described in ways which assume a one-to-one relationship in which, without pressure of time, a client is helped directly with her problem. This largely ignores the fact, however, that people are members of larger groups which exert strong influences on their behaviour and vice versa – the family is one such group.

A family's members both influence and are influenced by its organisation or structure. Thus, to be effective in working with families, counsellors need to be knowledgeable about both the dynamics of individual behaviour and the patterns of family interactions.

FAMILY ORGANISATION

There are a variety of family groupings: traditional nuclear families; single parent families; multi-generational families; blended or step-families (also called reconstituted, second chance, remarriage families); adoptive families. Despite these and other variations, however, for counselling purposes the family is best thought of as comprising all the members, including those who may not be present. Thus, where the parents are divorced the missing spouse is still considered to be a family member and may feature prominently in counselling. A deceased family member may also continue to exert influence on the family's functioning. Since relationships in family groupings are vitally important, individuals with no actual blood ties to the family may need to be thought of as 'family'. For example, a *de facto* partner or a notional 'aunt' or 'uncle' may actually function as central members in the family. Even pets may be thought of as family members. Families themselves are usually able to tell the counsellor who the members of their family are. Counsellors need to be aware that there will be cultural and gender-based variations in family composition. It is important to recognise such groupings as legitimate, and to overcome any biases one might have about the rightness or wrongness of such groupings.

All families, large or small, have rules for behaviour, roles that individual members typically play, methods for dealing with crises, and subgroupings of individual members. While these may be obvious to counsellors, many families will be unaware of them. Rules, for example, are tacitly agreed-upon behaviours that are usually adhered to by all family members. They may be explicit ('Bad language is not to be used in this household.') or implicit (the topic of sex is never mentioned in a particular family). Implicit rules are usually revealed by observing family interactions, or by asking family members about them directly. Families may have rules about who may talk to whom, what subjects may be openly discussed, how anger or love may be expressed. It can be helpful to note how rule-making and rule-enforcement are settled in a family. Useful insights can also be gained by noting the operating rules. Some rules are followed and openly talked about (eg, he has one night out a week); some are not talked about but are invariably followed (eg, she never drives the car when he is in it); some may be evident to any outsider but would probably be denied by those concerned (eg, she makes the major decisions).

Roles are patterns of behaviour that function to maintain the group or family and deal with problems that confront the family. For example, the father may play the role of disciplinarian and the mother the role of negotiator on behalf of the children; the eldest daughter may assume the role of protector of a younger sibling. A certain amount of role-playing and role-taking is inevitable in every family, but sometimes the roles adopted by or given to some members are so fixed that it becomes difficult for them to change – eg, clown, invalid, rebel, boss.

How a family deals with crises or challenges to its organisation is critical to its survival. Healthy families, for example, are able to respond to crises in ways that minimise disruption, or in more creative ways that may actually result in the family learning new ways of interacting. An example of the former is the healthy family's tacit acceptance of a teenage son's smoking. An example of a more creative solution to a crisis is a family's successful renegotiation of household roles and duties when the mother takes on a part-time, evening job. Coping methods in healthy, adaptive families tend to be characterised by flexibility, openness, and effective communication among their members. Dysfunctional or rigid families tend to cope with crises by imposing inflexible rules or codes of behaviour on their members. Responses that do not follow such rules pose too much of a threat to the family's stability and are therefore not allowed. An example would be a family's refusal to discuss or even acknowledge teenage sexuality, even after the daughter becomes pregnant. New, unusual responses to the crisis are not allowed. Dysfunctional families are characterised by ineffective communication, imposed rather than agreed-to rules, a feeling of hopelessness when faced with a crisis, and, often, a member who is the identified 'symptom carrier'. It is important to remember that it is not the crisis itself that defines the family, but rather, the family's response to the crisis. For example, when an argument between two family members develops, the adaptive family may actually learn from the conflict and change its pattern of interactions. On the other hand, the dysfunctional family will probably impose a solution on the conflict without regard for the needs of the individuals involved or the issue being discussed. The main aim will be to preserve the family status quo.

Subgroupings of individuals are the means through which families carry out the tasks necessary for their existence, eg, parenting, disciplining, earning, etc. Individuals can belong to different subgroups where they may play different roles and be subjected to different rules. Interactions among members of a subgroup may be on widely differing bases, eg, habitual, economic, supportive, sexual, persuasive, joking. Occasionally the boundaries between these subgroups become unclear or diffuse and effective family functioning breaks down.

There are several widely accepted reasons for working with family groups rather than individuals. They include:

1 Individuals must be considered in relation to their families. Families in turn must be seen as a part of several larger systems, for example neighbourhoods, communities, political or religious groupings.
2 Individuals are strongly influenced by and influence their families. Therefore, working with a person independent of her family ignores an important source of her psychological development.
3 It may be necessary to alter the family's patterns of interaction in order to change the behaviour of the individual members.

4 The identified client's problem usually affects the other family members as well. Usually when one member seeks help and is relieved of strain, others feel an increase in strain.

5 Other family members might gain a greater understanding of themselves and the family's patterns of interaction through sharing the problems of the identified client in the family grouping.

Family counselling is likely to be most effective when all members indicate a willingness to meet as a group with the counsellor; when all members express a concern and a willingness to accept some responsibility for improving the situation; when all members are motivated to continue living together as a family. There will be times, of course, when these conditions do not exist. However, family counselling may still succeed. For example, we do not believe that it is necessary for every member of the family to attend the counselling sessions. While the absence of a key family member may reduce the likelihood of successfully altering the family's system, it may still be productive – in fact necessary – to at least try to alleviate the family's suffering. Some members may attend reluctantly or refuse to accept any responsibility for the present situation. They may even try to subvert the counsellor's efforts to improve the family's interactions. Although these behaviours may make counselling more difficult, they are commonplace and represent the reality, rather than the ideal, of family counselling.

Family counselling is not likely to be effective when the parents are openly hostile toward and unco-operative with each other; when it is clear that one member needs individual counselling to resolve a personal dilemma, or enhance her self-esteem, or understand a personal developmental issue; when the problem only marginally affects other family members, such as the client's problems with her supervisor at work; when one or some of the family members are under threat of physical harm from another member.

In our experience many counsellors in a variety of settings (schools, welfare agencies, drop-in centres) express a desire to do family counselling but are hesitant and unsure about how to start and how to proceed once the family arrives. What follows, therefore, is a simple method for commencing family counselling, for analysing family structure and dysfunction and for changing the family's pattern of interaction in a planned, purposeful way. The method is problem-centred but it also incorporates thinking from the systems approach to family counselling.

We recommend that counsellors draw a 'diagnostic map' of the family's interaction patterns. A map or diagram of the family's structure is a way of organising and simplifying the wealth of information that is presented to the counsellor. The map serves several purposes: it helps the counsellor to organise his observations about the family in some clear, systematic way; it helps to construct or plan a series of homework tasks designed to change the family's patterns of relating to one another; it can be used to teach or illustrate certain points to the family itself. There have been various mapping strategies developed, most notably Murray Bowen's (1978) genograms and Salvadore Minuchin's (1974) structural maps. Whatever method is used, the intention is the same: organising information into some clear, meaningful form. Below is a sample diagnostic map based on the family described in Exercise 2 at the end of this chapter. The mapping system used is Minuchin's. It is essential to have a clear picture of the family's relationships before implementing solutions or prescribing homework tasks designed to change the family's patterns of relating to one another.

FIGURE 7.1 DIAGNOSTIC MAP OF THE SMITH FAMILY

$$\frac{M = F}{S \quad J}$$

On the basis of the information given, the mother and father have formed a coalition against the identified problem, John. John's relationship with Sue is, as yet, unknown.

FIGURE 7.2 SYMBOLS

(Counsellors can use conventional symbols or create their own.)

}   Coalition: two or more family members united around an issue.

-++-   Conflict between individuals or family subsystems.

. . . .   Diffuse or unclear boundaries between subsystems.

=   Affiliation: a clearly agreed upon alliance between two individuals.

— Rigid boundary between subsystems.

--- Clear boundary between subsystems.

≡ Overinvolvement between family members.

STAGES OF FAMILY COUNSELLING

1 The referral

When a client approaches a counsellor for help, the initial discussion may indicate clearly that the client's problem involves her family and that a satisfactory individual solution to the problem is unlikely. At that point the counsellor must convince the client that family counselling would be productive. This may be accomplished by pointing out to the client that other family members may have differing views of the problem and that by sharing these a fuller picture of the problem may be gained, that others will be affected by the problem and may also need help or support, and that the family may need a third party to help them see new ways of coping with the problem. Following that, one of two courses of action can be followed: (a) the client can be left to persuade the family to be present for counselling, or (b) the counsellor, with the client's permission, can contact the rest of the family to explain the need for counselling and arrange the initial appointment. In either case, it is important that a firm commitment to be present is gained from as many members as possible and that a specific time, day, and place to meet are arranged. Usually the counselling will occur in the counsellor's office, but there may be times when counselling will take place in the family's home or in some other place unfamiliar to the counsellor.

Some counsellors believe it is best if the client negotiates with the family and gains their commitment to be present for counselling. We have no such preference. Rather, when family counselling is indicated, we think it is more important that the family is actually present for the initial interview. Who makes the initial arrangements is of secondary importance.

These initial contacts are, however, the beginning of family counselling. Who asks for help, how he/she describes the problem, who negotiates with the rest of the family members, what is said to them regarding the reason for family counselling, which members are eventually present for the first session, where counselling actually takes place — all of these things can be revealing of the family's patterns of communication, and the rules and roles that govern members' behaviour.

2 Introduction, greetings

Depending on where the counselling takes place, the counsellor's role in greeting the family may differ. If, for example, counselling takes place in the family's – or a relative's – home, the counsellor will need to be aware of the family's cultural background and how that may affect the rules and rituals of meeting and greeting. The counsellor may find himself being welcomed into the home in some formal way. In any case, the counsellor should observe the customs of the family with whom he is working. For example, in some homes it may be a sign of respect to leave one's shoes at the door, to greet the eldest family members first, or to eat and drink something before engaging in more serious matters. Dress is also important; so too is the language used. Both should be sensible and reflect the counsellor's sensitivity to the family's customary habits and values.

If the counselling is to take place in the counsellor's office, it is still imperative to be aware of and observe the family's customary greetings. In this situation it is the counsellor who is playing host to the family and each family member should be acknowledged either verbally or non-verbally in a culturally appropriate way. Names should be used, both the counsellor's and those of the family members. Counsellors need to take a few extra minutes if need be to meet and greet each family member as an individual. Common courtesy and greeting rituals should be observed. This may include some amount of culturally appropriate small-talk.

Whatever the setting, rapport-building, also called joining, represents the counsellor's attempt to blend with the family's style, background, and values. This requires careful attention to the family's actions, seating arrangements, and language. By this stage the counsellor will have already gathered significant information about the family's structure and patterns of interaction. This information includes aspects of the initial referral and what can be observed as the first session begins (How does each family member greet the counsellor? How do they seat themselves? Who speaks first? What is the mood or climate of the family?).

Remember, even in this early stage of counselling the counsellor becomes part of the family system, another member of the group. There may be early attempts by some family members to oppose the counsellor. For example, an antagonistic adolescent may see the counsellor as just another critical adult and therefore refuse to trust and interact with him. Some may try to collude with the counsellor against another family member. The parents, for example, may try to get the counsellor to join them in blaming their 'problem child'. The counsellor needs to be aware of these dynamics and be able to work constructively with them.

The Smith Family:

At the first interview the counsellor observed that the parents and Sue sat side by side in the waiting room. John sat by himself across the room. As the counsellor invited them into his office, he noticed that John entered last, reluctantly. There was obvious tension among the family members and Mrs Smith seemed tense and tight-lipped. When the counsellor had greeted each person and invited them to seat themselves, the following pattern emerged:

FIGURE 7.3 SEATING ARRANGEMENTS FOR THE FIRST INTERVIEW

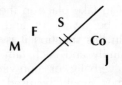

John, the identified problem, was isolated from the rest of the family. The counsellor chose to sit next to him to convey support and acceptance.

3 Structuring time

At the first counselling session it is useful to discuss the practicalities or terms of counselling. For example, both the counsellor and the family members should know at the outset how much time is available for each session. This helps both parties to work more effectively within the time allowed and makes transitions from one topic or interviewing phase to another seem less abrupt, more explicable.

Placing time limits on the session and making those limits explicit to all involved can build positive expectations regarding process and outcome in family members: (a) change can and will begin almost immediately; (b) families need not be dependent on counsellors for extended periods of time – they can be and are expected to resolve their own problems. While positive expectations regarding counselling are not in themselves sufficient to ensure successful outcomes, the role of client expectations in counselling has long been recognised and documented.

It may be desirable at this point to set some guidelines about confidentiality, about each person having the right to speak, and about the need to allow individuals to have differing views. It may also be useful to decide to meet for a set number of sessions, for example two, before deciding how and whether to proceed.

4 Problem definition

As soon as the family has been greeted and is feeling more comfortable, each member's view of the family's problem is sought. Even though one individual may be the identified problem, it may be stressed that the problem is a family problem: 'When one person misbehaves (is troubled) it usually affects the whole family in some way. How do you think this misbehaviour (problem) is affecting your family?' This reinforces the notion that the problem is a shared problem and warrants the efforts of the entire family to solve it. It is useful to find out what each member knows about why the family has come for counselling. Thus, the counsellor can begin with a simple question like 'I would like to hear from each of you what brings the family here today'. This information is added to that already received (see Stage 2) to continue building and modifying the 'diagnostic map' of the family's interaction patterns.

Family counsellors should allow all family members time to speak about things from their own point of view. This might mean they will have to be more directive and active than they might normally be. Counsellor interventions at this stage should be tentative probes designed to test the family's structure, or reveal more about the family's rules, roles, boundaries, and organisational structure. A probe may take the form of a direct question about a sensitive topic, a change in seating to bring people together or move them apart, or a set task to see how well family members work together (for example, have them plan a weekend outing together).

Family problems usually show up as breakdowns in communication. Sometimes this is due to an absence of suitable models: some people cannot imagine family members disagreeing without the interchange sinking into fruitless argument. Many other factors may contribute to poor communication in a family. One parent may have a pressing problem; both parents may have rigid and unrealistic ideas about children's behaviour or school work; there may be understandable worries about adolescents' experimenting with cars, alcohol, and sex; some may have strong desires to control young people's careers or religious beliefs.

Where communications are unsatisfactory, the counsellor can help a great deal by directing all members to talk to one another in new ways. Essentially, the counsellor intervenes to give directions in the form of simple rules. He may ask that all members follow these rules when they want to sort out a difficulty with others in the family.

The following rules are often useful, both as an aid to problem assessment and as a means of altering the family's present organisation. It can also be pointed out to the family that following these rules can improve their future communication patterns.

1 Do not talk *about* people who are present. Talk *to* them, look at them while you are talking, and use their names.
2 Say what you want to say directly but try to be positive. As well as telling others what you want them to stop doing, say what it is that you would like them to do instead.
3 Whenever possible, talk about problems and feelings as they arise. Tell others how you feel. Do not bottle up feelings of resentment, and do not pretend things are all right when they are not.
4 When others are talking to you, hear them out. Do not interrupt or try to stop them saying certain things. Furthermore, listen carefully to all that is being said to you, especially when the talk is about feelings.
5 Tell others what you like about what they do, as they do it, or as soon as possible afterwards. Emphasise the good things.

FIGURE 7.4 PROBLEM DEFINITION IN THE SMITH FAMILY

As the parents described the problem, it became clear that the parents held similar views: John was the source of the family's difficulties. John was 'under fire' from both parents and said he felt picked on. He expressed the desire 'to be left alone'.

Fig 7.4a

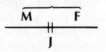

When Sue was asked for her view of the situation, new information emerged. She, too, felt distanced from her parents ('They never pay any real attention to me. They are only interested in whether I'm being "good" and doing well at school.'). She felt some sympathy for John. This new information was incorporated into the map, as shown below:

Fig 7.4b

At this point the counsellor decided to split the parental co-alition and bring John closer to the family centre by changing seats with the mother. The counsellor surmised that she was less dominant over and hostile toward John than was the father. Changing seats with the mother also extricated the counsellor from a go-between role and put the mother in the position of potential mediator.

The new diagram incorporating these moves is shown below. Note that the simple act of changing seats was designed to alter the family dynamics and to test out certain hypotheses about the family structure. The seating became:

Fig 7.4c

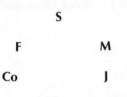

5 Solutions

Once all members have had an opportunity to describe the problem as they see it, it is useful to ask for each person's opinion about how to solve or alleviate the problem: 'What does each of you think would make things in the family better than they are now?' Again, the focus is on the family's solution to the family's problems. This information serves two main purposes: (a) it gives the counsellor further information about the family's structure and interactional patterns, and hence the diagnostic map becomes more detailed and well defined; (b) it gives the counsellor some indication about how to intervene in or restructure the family by means of homework.

It is important to know what solutions have been tried in the past and what is being tried at present. The counsellor should listen for repetitive patterns in the family's solutions (eg, punishments, ignoring the problem) to gain some understanding of what has failed, what has succeeded, and what should be avoided when assigning homework. It may well be that at this point in the family's development the most productive interventions are likely to be those things that have not been tried, those that are new, fresh, creative. The 'more of the same' approach will usually fail.

FIGURE 7.5

Having completed the first task with the Smith Family (ascertaining each person's view of the family's problem), the second is introduced: 'What would make things in the family better?' Note that the focus is on the *family*, not just John.

a. Sue's comments indicated a split with her parents, especially her mother:

Fig 7.5a

$$M \neq S$$

b. Mrs Smith felt picked on by the whole family. She wanted John to behave and desired a closer relationship with Sue:

Fig 7.5b   Fig 7.5c

Real: F ——M—— ⫽   Ideal: F = M
              S : J   - - - - - - - -
                                                  S = J

c. Mr Smith continued to see John as *the problem*:

Fig 7.5d

d. John repeated his plea for the family to just leave him alone.

Fig 7.5e

M   F   S
_____
J

6 Therapeutic suggestions or homework

Having mentally constructed a diagnostic map of the family and heard how each member would like things changed, the counsellor negotiates homework tasks (see Homework, Chapter Five, p 90) with various family members. The tasks must be designed to alter the family's usual ways of interacting with one another. Carrying out homework tasks extends counselling into the home and, if effectively chosen, challenges the family to adapt and alter – if only in small ways – their dysfunctional patterns.

Homework must be realistic (something within the family's capabilities), must be a small enough step to encourage the family to attempt it, and must involve those who are initially most amenable or receptive (to enhance chances of success). When the family members perform the homework and find the results preferable to the old patterns, there is the strong possibility that they will continue to change in other ways and be more willing to undergo additional counselling sessions. Therefore, it is important that the homework is achievable so the family can experience the confidence that comes with success.

Once the homework tasks are given, the counsellor should gain a commitment from those involved that they will actually carry them out. Often families need a rationale for what they are being asked to do, reasons for attempting new behaviours. Basically, the task needs to be 'sold' to the family members. Two useful strategies to accomplish this are to have the various family members summarise what they are to do (this checks their understanding of the homework task), and to have them say aloud that they are willing to carry out the task (this serves as a public commitment to act).

FIGURE 7.6 HOMEWORK FOR THE SMITH FAMILY

After hearing each member's views about what would make things in the family better, the counsellor began to alter the family interaction. First, he directed the father and John to negotiate a new relationship. Both had hinted that each would like to be close to the other again, but neither seemed able to initiate the change. So, in order to simultaneously lessen the strength of the parents' coalition and to boost the mother's self-esteem and confidence in the family, the counsellor directed the mother to act as mediator as her husband and son decided how to get along more amicably.

This manoeuvre is shown below:

Fig 7.6a   Fig 7.6b

becomes

After the father and John agreed – with the mother's help and guidance – to go fishing the next weekend, the counsellor then directed the mother and Sue to negotiate a new, more satisfying way of interacting. Subsequently, they agreed to spend at least 15 minutes together each evening talking about things of mutual interest (eg, school, hobbies, etc.). Thus, the family map became:

Fig 7.6c

$$
\begin{array}{c|c}
M & F \\
\| & \| \\
S & J
\end{array}
$$

NOTE: The counsellor's interventions were designed to accomplish three things:
1 to enhance Mrs Smith's status in the family;
2 to bring John and his father closer together by involving them in an agreed-upon, pleasurable activity (fishing);
3 to encourage the mother and Sue to spend time together.

All of these interventions worked to diminish the strength of the parents' coalition against the identified problem, John, and replaced this coalition with new, more constructive relationships between the mother and daughter and the father and John. The relationship between Sue and John remained unclear and unaltered. The counsellor had decided that the children's relationship could be explored in a later session if that proved necessary.

7 Terminating
Once the homework has been discussed and agreed to, the session can be terminated. Termination can be initiated by reviewing what has been accomplished and reiterating each person's new responsibilities. A follow-up contact is negotiated.

Some family counsellors believe that counselling should be on a once-per-week basis. We suggest that this frequency may be necessary only with highly disturbed, tenuously connected families. For most families a two or three-week break may be more productive. This longer period of time will allow the family to adjust to the new patterns of interacting imposed by the homework task, to work out new roles and rules in response to the altered family dynamics. If it seems necessary to check on the family's progress during the two-week interval, the counsellor can assign one of the family members to ring him to report on the family's progress. This contact will keep the family in counselling without the necessity of an actual counselling session.

FIGURE 7.7

After the negotiations among the various Smith Family members were completed, the counsellor summarised (a) what had been done, and (b) what each person had agreed to do. One final task he presented to the family was for them to decide which one of them would ring him in a week's time to report on how things were going. This served to reinforce the lessening of the parental coalition and demanded that the family discuss whose responsibility it was to report on *the whole family's progress*, not just John's behaviour. The aim was to build more appropriate boundaries among all four family members:

Fig 7.7

BRIEF FAMILY COUNSELLING

Many counsellors in a variety of settings have reported to us that it is often unrealistic to expect families to commit themselves to anything more than two to three counselling sessions. The method of family counselling outlined above can be usefully employed with such families. Counsellors doing brief family counselling must, however, develop their diagnostic skills (use of a co-counsellor helps in learning these skills), and they should be prepared to be more active and directive than they might ordinarily be. If time is limited, it must be carefully managed to ensure that the entire process just described is covered. This type of brief counselling, while not necessarily ideal, recognises the fact that some families will not commit themselves to multiple-session counselling and gives the counsellor a simple, structured plan for managing the session and increasing the likelihood of impacting on families in a significant way.

One or two-session family counselling can be extended by arranging telephone contact at a later date. This keeps the family 'in counselling' and the importance of the homework can be reinforced (see Figure 7.7, above). In fact, who is chosen to contact the counsellor can be part of the therapeutic intervention. For example, the uninvolved, ignored father could be asked to ring the counsellor in a week's time to report how the family has been progressing. Another useful way of doing this is to have the family decide among themselves who will ring the counsellor. Thus, by assigning family members homework tasks and arranging a telephone follow-up contact, one or two-session counselling can be extended considerably.

EXERCISES:

1 Using your own family of origin, draw a diagnostic map of its organisation. Note the rules and roles that operated in your family. Describe how crises or challenges were dealt with. What subgroups existed and what functions did they serve?

2 Use the following brief description of a family in difficulty in an extended role-play. Other family situations from your own experience can be used as well:
The Smith family has two children: John, aged 14, and Sue, aged 12. Mr Smith rang the counsellor for help because John had been involved with two other boys in shoplifting. There have been three previous incidents of John stealing money from his father and sister and from Scout funds. In all of these incidents Mr Smith had 'covered up' for his son. Earlier in life John was quite conforming, but in the last twelve months has grown increasingly sullen and withdrawn. The latest shoplifting incident has come as a shock and disappointment to both parents.
Sue, on the other hand, is well-behaved and fits the parent's expectations very well. She does well at school and is often praised at home for being such a 'good helper' to her mother. John is viewed as the 'black sheep' of the family. The Smiths own a small grocer's shop. The father works long hours and takes great pride in his upright, honest character. Both parents have made great sacrifices to provide well for their children.
Mrs Smith supports her husband in impressing on the children the importance of intellectual achievement, moral standards, the value of hard work, and the need to give up immediate pleasure for future reward. She works part-time in a chemist's shop to supplement the earnings from the grocery.

John seems selfish, self-centred, lazy, and unmotivated in school. He is often unco-operative at home and refuses to spend time with the family at weekends. A neighbour occasionally takes him fishing – he loves the outdoors. This man seems to be his only friend.

(a) Assign various people to role-play the parts of the four family members. Allow them time to discuss their role and the family's dilemma so that they have an understanding of and feeling for the family's dynamics.

(b) Assign two people to be co-counsellors. Role-play the family counselling sequence as outlined in this chapter. The same role-play can extend over several training sessions, each approximating a typical family counselling session. At the end of each session family members and counsellors should discuss what has happened and why. The counsellors' efforts can be constructively critiqued and new goals discussed for the next role-play session. This exercise can be repeated several times using different role-players.

(c) To practise Brief Family Counselling compress the several-session sequence into one, paying particular attention to the structuring of time and the assignment of homework. At the end of the session discuss as described above.

8

Consultation

One-to-one remedial counselling is limited in its scope to the problems of an individual. However, through consultation, a counsellor can reach more people, contribute to institutional change and assume a preventative role.

INTRODUCTION

Consultation is a helping process whereby the counsellor-consultant and those consulting, treating each other as equals and respecting each other's skill and expertise, work together to solve a problem or institute change. The consultant works with the key personnel in an organisation to advise them on how to help particular clients or how to change the system in ways which will help individual members in it. Through training and self-awareness the counsellor has skills in communication and interpersonal relationships which equip her to act as a good consultant and to deal with the feelings that arise when changes are instituted.

The effective counsellor-consultant should be open-minded, skilled in relating to others and able to share power in a relationship of equality and mutual respect.

She should be knowledgeable about the consultation process, the change process, and the nature of organisations, in particular the one to which she is going.

Consulting requires skill in assessment, problem-solving, decision-making, negotiation, planning, evaluation, and effective use of resources.

An example of consultation would be a school principal calling on a psychologist to diagnose a pupil's problem and advise the teacher on how to deal with it. In this situation it is essential that the psychologist-consultant obtain accurate and full information from as many sources as possible. She may directly observe the client in the setting of concern or arrange for some third person to systematically record teacher-pupil interactions.

It is essential that the consultant communicates clearly with the principal and teacher so that they understand her role and their roles, how she assesses the problem, what actions she sees as feasible and what outcomes can be expected. It is also most important to check on progress and evaluate the final outcome.

Through the consultation process the psychologist-consultant shares her expertise by modelling, and involving the teacher in, the processes of problem-definition, generation of solutions, and evaluation of results. Indirectly she 'treats' an individual client by allowing a teacher to be in direct control of the helping process. The teacher selects the methods he thinks are the most appropriate from those suggested, he determines the best timing, he carries out the treatment, and he decides when he is satisfied.

TYPES OF CONSULTATION

Providing an expert service

The consultant and the consultee together gather information and define the problem but the consultant assumes responsibility for carrying out the selected intervention. This may involve training others. For example a factory manager may feel that his supervisors lack skill in communicating with the workers for whom they are responsible. A school principal may want to appoint deans within a pastoral care network but may feel that the teachers selected need some training before undertaking their new role. In both situations a counsellor-consultant could provide training in communication skills. Such training is in demand in church and education groups, commercial, industrial, and retailing firms and voluntary social agencies as well as in the professional helping services.

Prescribing a remedy

The consultant acts as a resource person, assisting in diagnosis and suggesting a remedy. A parent may consult a counsellor about a disobedient teenager, a wife may consult about how to help her alcoholic husband or an employee may seek assistance on how to help workmates cope with a domineering supervisor.

Mediating

The consultation process starts with the consultant, who upon becoming aware of a problem, gathers and analyses information, makes a case for change and then presents it to those who are influential in the situation. Most of us are resistant to change and so the consultant may have to be a catalyst or motivator.

A school guidance counsellor could assume this role when made aware of growing numbers of new entrants with learning disabilities. She could gather data to illustrate the extent of the problem, present this to the principal and heads of departments and propose ways of providing remedial services.

Collaborating

Within an egalitarian relationship the consultant shares skill and expertise in a way that enhances the consultee's ability to work on the problem. This involves diagnosing it, gathering information, proposing, selecting, and implementing solutions and evaluating results.

The example of a social studies teacher asking a guidance counsellor for help illustrates the collaborative type of consultation.

THE CONSULTATION PROCESS

As illustrated in the diagram in Figure 8.1, there are eleven stages in the consultation process. While it is helpful to set them out in this way the stages may occur out of sequence or be repeated. For example the consultant may be required to establish relationships with new people at several points in the process, and information may need to be gathered to help in the diagnosis stage, in choosing a solution, and in evaluation.

If the consultant's first task is to raise awareness she will be adopting a mediating role. If she is to provide training as one of the solutions she is delivering an expert service.

What is involved in each stage is elaborated later. The sections on preparation and making contact fit into the third stage, Establishment of a Relationship.

FIGURE 8.1

THE CONSULTATION PROCESS

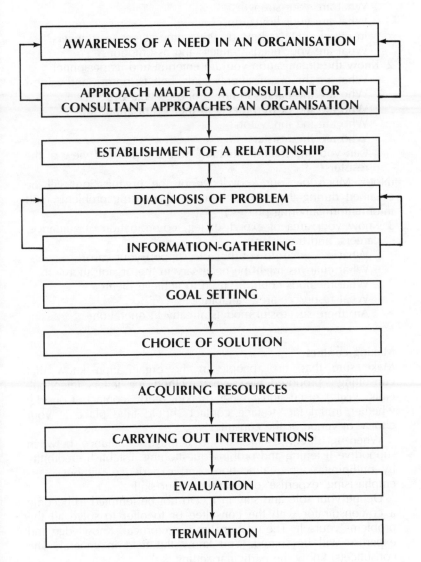

ELABORATION OF THE CONSULTATION PROCESS

Preparation
1 Know yourself:
   What are your strengths?
   What are your limitations?
   In initial contacts how do you come across to strangers?
   What are your needs, values, and assumptions?
2 Know the organisation you are entering and its personnel:
   What are the organisation's goals, beliefs, norms, and values?
   Who are the clients in any proposed change?
   Who are the powerbrokers in the organisation?
   Who are the innovators?
   Who are the resisters?
   Can you analyse the situation from the point of view of the resisters?
(Note: Much of your knowledge of the organisation will be obtained during the making contact, diagnosing problems, and information-gathering phases.)
3 Know your area of expertise: (eg, co-ordination of guidance, careers, and transition)
   What evidence do you have to support your case?
   What changes might be necessary in the organisation?
   What methods could be used to achieve them?
   What resources are available?
   Are there successful models already in operation?

Making contact
Make sure that most people in the organisation know that consulting is proposed. Use several methods (eg, letters, telephone calls, visits, discussions) when making early contact. Consider whether initial face-to-face contact should take place at your choice of venue or the consultee's.

When in direct contact try to achieve a balance between supportive listening and probing questioning. Establish credibility by outlining your qualifications and experience without over-emphasising 'expertise' or devaluing your skills.

Define your role and stay in it. Do not be tempted to become a co-conspirator with the consultee or to offer to solve all the problems yourself. The relationship is reciprocal. Knowledge and expertise will be shared. You know the field in general. The consultee(s) know the particular setting.

Finally, you should obtain an initial statement of the problem which focuses on issues and set some boundaries. The following questions will assist you to do this:

1 What is the aim of any intervention?
2 What specific responsibilities will the consultant assume?
3 Who else will be involved?
4 What will be their responsibilities?
5 Will all this be specified in writing?
6 What time span is anticipated?
7 Who will pay any costs?
8 How should results be reported?
9 To whom will results be available?
10 Will the results be published as research?
11 To what extent should proceedings be confidential?

Diagnosing problems

Be aware that the presenting and underlying problems may be different. For example a supervisor may consult a counsellor on the best way to discuss with an employee who has a disability that his work is deficient and his social behaviour is irritating. Further investigation may reveal that the job specification is inadequate and that the employee has not been given feedback by those with whom he works that his chatter interrupts their concentration. They may have been unable to give such feedback because their feelings of guilt or discomfort in relation to people with disabilities prevent them from being honest.

Through questioning of the consultee identify problems, strengths, and opportunities in the organisation. Identify the key people in it.

Establish realistic goals and consider any possible constraints on achieving them.

Consider whether more information is required. If this is so, the problem may need to be redefined later.

Gathering information

Information should provide a basis for action. It should not by its nature alienate the consultee nor should it alienate those from whom it is sought.

The required information may already be available. If not, define the purposes for which new information may be required. Is it needed to convince people, to define a need, or to provide baseline data against which to evaluate progress?

Methods of obtaining information include:

1 Listening to the consultee and other people in the organisation.
2 Observation.
3 Questionnaires. These must be appropriate for the target group. Issues such as the possibility of reading difficulties need to be considered.
4 Structured interviews.
5 Group meetings. A method of using these is outlined:
   (a) A key question is asked.
   (b) Participants privately write down their ideas.
   (c) The ideas are pooled without discussion of them.
   (d) There is then open discussion.
   (e) Participants privately rank ideas.
   (f) The overall ranking is collated and considered.

When gathering information other considerations include the possibility of bias, ownership of the data, and methods of presenting it.

Setting goals and objectives
Goals are general statements of intent, eg, to achieve effective co-ordination of guidance, careers, and transition activities at Aoraki High School.
Objectives are statements specifying meaningful, obtainable, measurable outcomes, eg, appoint a co-ordinator.
Consider whether the goals and objectives are clear and specific and whether they have been obtained by consensus. Does everyone understand them and what they imply?
A Test for Consensus
1 Can everyone paraphrase the goals to show understanding of them?
2 Has everyone had a chance to express feelings about the goals and objectives?
3 Are those who disagree willing to publicly accept a majority decision and give the proposal a trial?
Consideration should also be given as to whether the organisation has the resources, skills, and money to implement the goals, whether they are flexible enough to be changed if circumstances change and whether there are ways of rewarding people who achieve them.

Choosing a solution
Generate ideas by brainstorming (Note: preclude criticism of any ideas at this stage).
Evaluate each solution in relation to the objectives.
Evaluate in relation to practicality, benefit, and diffusibility.
Does the organisation have the people and financial resources needed?
Do the staff have the necessary skills or will they need training?
Will students, teachers, and administrators be rewarded by carrying out these solutions?
What are the implications of using the chosen solutions?

Acquiring resources
Resources need to be readily accessible, relevant, and not costly. Standardised tests, questionnaires, checklists, and structured interviews may be used in diagnosis. Policy statements, reading lists, and guest speakers may be used to raise awareness. It may be possible to try out some resources in a pilot study or to obtain feedback about their value from previous users.
You may use paper, people, film, video or audio resources.

Carrying out interventions
It is helpful to consider the following questions:

1 How are you going to implement change?
2 Who will be responsible for each aspect?
3 Within what time span do you hope to achieve change?
4 What methods will you use?
    simulation exercises
    films or videos
    outside speakers
    observation
    exposition
    modelling
    research exercises
    worksheets
    feedback from participants
    interaction in pairs, threes, or small groups
    planning exercises
    case studies
    set reading

skill-learning and practice (on video, in the actual situation, in simulations)
workshops
role-playing
lectures
observation
resource sharing
visits
discussion
5 Is there a clear understanding of job specifications?
6 Is there an adequate division of labour?
7 Is the change process co-ordinated?

Evaluating

It is at this stage that outcomes should be measured. Go back to the objectives and consider whether you will evaluate formally through the use of questionnaires, checklists or structured interviews, or by observation. The evaluation may also be done through informal discussion with staff, students, and where relevant, parents.

The following questions can be asked.

1 Which of the objectives have been met?
2 What has not worked?
3 Is it necessary to redefine problems?
4 Should new strategies be tried?
5 Should there be formal reporting back?
6 To whom and in what form?

Terminating

The conditions under which termination is to occur should be specified in the initial contract.

When there is evidence that goals have been met and that the organisation is able to carry on without further support, termination should occur. A later follow-up may be proposed.

DEALING WITH RESISTANCE

Resistance will be lessened if participants see proposed changes as reducing rather than increasing their stress and if what is proposed fits in with their values and ideals. Participants who are involved in the diagnosis and definition of the problem are less likely to feel that their autonomy and security are threatened. The chance to take part in an interesting new experience can act as an incentive.

As change takes place, resistance will be reduced if the feelings of participants are acknowledged and opposing viewpoints are heard and respected. Relationships based on acceptance, trust, support, and where appropriate, confidentiality, contribute to the lessening of resistance.

The programme and the organisers need to be flexible and open to feedback. Where agreement is reached by consensus there is more chance of commitment to change.

EFFECTIVENESS OF CONSULTATION

Achievement of the specified outcomes is not the only criterion for judging the effectiveness of consultation. Other valid outcomes of consultation include the provision of accurate, up-to-date information to an organisation and the bringing into the open of aspects of it that may have been denied or hidden.

Experiencing a reciprocal relationship benefits the consultee and the consultant. The consultee learns some skills in problem-definition, decision-making, planning and communication, and has the satisfaction of being able to make his/her own commitment to change. There is also the satisfaction that comes from being fully involved in the consultation process.

QUESTIONS TO ASK WHEN CHOOSING A CONSULTANT

1 Why do we require the services of a consultant?
2 What is it possible to achieve within the limitations imposed by our organisational structure?
3 Do we want a neutral chairperson or referee from outside the organisation?
4 Do we want someone with particular expertise to act as a catalyst or an analyst?
5 Do we want someone to assist with the formalising of a system?
6 Do we want someone to teach new skills?
7 What resources does the organisation need to supply to the consultant? (eg, organisational policy, list of personnel etc.)
8 What preparation does the organisation need to do?
9 What should happen after the consultation has ended?
10 What evaluation and follow-up should take place?

The consultant may come from inside or outside the organisation. An insider will be familiar with the system but may not be able to achieve enough independence, objectivity, and status to be acceptable and effective. An outsider, while not knowing the organisation intimately, can come in with a fresh perspective, objectivity, and independence of the power structure.

AN EXAMPLE OF A CONSULTATION
A Social Studies Teacher Asks a Guidance Counsellor for Help
At Aoraki High School, social studies teachers choose form 4 topics which illustrate the theme Social Change. If they wish, they may include a unit on the World of Work.

Mrs Barnett, teacher of a low average fourth form, approached Mr Bracewell, the guidance counsellor, for help in incorporating some careers work into her social studies programme. She felt her students were likely to be early leavers, they seemed to know little about the world of work and they had expressed interest in finding out more. Thus a teacher, aware of a need among her students, approached a guidance counsellor to act as consultant.

Mr Bracewell invited Mrs Barnett to meet him in his office after school and to bring her scheme of work with her. During discussion he helped her to clarify her goals and objectives. She wanted to raise awareness and in particular to emphasise the changing role of women, the changes produced in the workforce by the introduction of new technology, and the implications of rising unemployment. A relationship was established and the problem specified.

Mr Bracewell suggested that Mrs Barnett get each class member to list in order of preference three possible career choices. In the meantime he would assemble a number of useful teacher and student resources. They agreed to meet again on Friday after school. Thus stage five of the consultation process, namely information-gathering, was completed.

When Mr Bracewell saw the lists he suggested that one objective should be to widen student choices. This would be particularly important for the girls, two-thirds of whom had chosen hairdressing as first preference. He further suggested that the students be confronted with some of the realities of the employment situation. Goals had now been set.

It was agreed to start from where the students were by summarising their preferences and presenting the summary to them. Mr Bracewell agreed to teach the first lesson. He proposed to make a pie graph of student preferences on an overhead transparency and to compare that with the destinations of Aoraki High School leavers and with New Zealand school leavers as a whole. Students would be encouraged to change choices if their initial ones looked unrealistic.

With Mrs Barnett, students would then investigate a job of their choice, widen this to look at career families, assess their suitability for the chosen jobs, learn to use the Careers Information Service leaflets in the library and look at the issues of women at work, technology, and unemployment. Jointly, the teacher and counsellor-consultant had chosen solutions which they later implemented.

Mr Bracewell provided Mrs Barnett with the pamphlet *Women in the Workforce*, the latest unemployment figures from the *Labour and Employment Gazette* and an article on new technology from the *Vocational Guidance Bulletin*. He introduced her to the *Looking Ahead* material for use with the class and provided a class set of job scenes and a set of blank brieflets for students to complete. After school on Tuesday he demonstrated to her how to use the CIS leaflets in the library. Thus resources were acquired.

The lessons were taught as agreed, the students filled in a brief evaluation of the unit and the consultant, Mr Bracewell, discussed the results with Mrs Barnett. It was agreed that later in the term she would repeat the unit with a high ability class and that Mr Bracewell would provide extension material for that. Evaluation and termination completed the consultation process.

THE COUNSELLOR-CONSULTANT AS TRAINER

Any organisation contemplating major change will have to consider its communication systems. A counsellor could well adopt a consultant role by teaching a communication skills course. In some respects such training may become a form of group counselling for the participants on the training course. Participants have personal goals in entering into training and they have the opportunity for open sharing of feelings and for honest feedback. They can grow in self-awareness and in understanding of others through the relationships established during the training. Such learning, of course, is also open to the training course leader as she receives feedback from participants. She should make it clear that she, too, is willing and expecting to learn.

CLARITY OF AIMS AND OBJECTIVES

It is vital that aims and objectives be clearly specified as a means of structuring and directing a course. Teaching communication skills demands a high level of leader and participant involvement and is much more difficult than imparting information in a lecture situation. It is very easy to lose or confuse the participants. Clearly stated aims and objectives help to provide a sense of security, direction, purpose, and progress, all of which encourage involvement.

In the first place it is necessary for those desiring training to state their aims clearly and precisely. They may need help to do this as their starting point may have been vague. It may take time to get people to state aims but during the process the person who will be their leader can become aware of their stage of development. The following questions may be useful:

1 When, and for how long, are sessions to be held?
2 How many people will be involved?
3 What facilities are available?
4 What sort of training have participants been involved in before, if any?
5 What is the spread of ages and education?
6 What would you hope each participant would learn?
7 What overall effect do you hope for in your organisation?
8 What sort of follow-up, if any, is planned?

It must be emphasised that the structure of the course, the explanations, and the selection of practical exercises should all serve to further the aims and objectives. Otherwise activities may be but pleasant time-fillers. Participants may be invited to prepare for the course by reading certain material, filling in questionnaires or engaging in some form of self-analysis. Finally, when the course is under way, participants are entitled to know the aims of the whole course and the expected learnings from each exercise. Also, they should have the opportunity to provide feedback as to how far the aims and objectives have been achieved. In skills training the emphasis should be on practical exercises with a minimum of theory and a maximum of involvement. However, there is content and that content should be illustrated by the exercises and summarised by the leader afterwards.

SIZE AND COMPOSITION OF GROUPS

Various factors need to be considered when deciding on group size. The amount of space available may place a limit on numbers. If physical arrangements are adequate, a group of 20–24 can be handled comfortably by one leader provided the group subdivides where appropriate. Some practical exercises call for pairs, others for threes and yet others for fours. Experience suggests a group membership of six to ten (with eight the preferred number) is most appropriate for discussions or small group interactions.

When the composition of a group is considered, differences in sex, age, educational level, ability to verbalise, and personality may be significant. Drawing attention to issues or problems that may result from these differences can provide effective teaching points for the group leader. If, for example, group members are threatened by the presence of a university graduate, this issue should be revealed and aired. The feelings aroused may be similar to those a client experiences when meeting 'an expert', eg, a counsellor. This similarity can be emphasised to the group.

There seems to be no optimum combination of characteristics. Diversity in the group provides varying points of view. In the end the significant features usually turn out to be the degree of commitment to the training course, willingness to share openly and to change, and the ability to accept and deal with one's own reactions and those of others.

VOLUNTARY OR INVOLUNTARY MEMBERSHIP

This issue in relation to counselling individual clients has already been examined in Chapter Three. Voluntary membership is usually preferable. The negative feelings or defensiveness of an involuntary group member may have a powerful dampening effect. If the situation is particularly threatening to the involuntary member, he may even set out deliberately to sabotage proceedings. The involuntary member may also convey his negative feelings to outsiders and thus prejudice them against such forms of training.

Besides the danger to the group there is also potential danger for the involuntary member. A number of people who appear to function well in ordinary life may really be hiding behind a mask. Open sharing in a group may force this mask off and leave the participant without the help and support needed to deal with his feeling of being exposed.

As with the involuntary client in individual counselling, it is important to raise the issue of compulsory participation if the organisation you are helping has insisted on it. We believe that a person with strong negative feelings towards training should be given the chance to withdraw. But, if at the outset the invited leader suggests to the organisation that voluntary participation is preferred, the issue need not arise. Once the course begins, however, voluntary participants may find themselves reacting very defensively because they could not have realised previously the extent to which the activities would be threatening. Such negative feelings should be dealt with as they arise and not be put aside.

THE PHYSICAL SETTING

The physical setting should be as comfortable and relaxing as possible. The room temperature needs to be warm enough for comfort but not so warm that it will send everyone to sleep. There should be as little as possible outside interference in the form of extraneous noise or interruptions. Traffic noise or noise from other rooms that are not sound-proofed can be distracting. A carpeted or carpet-tiled room, comfortable chairs, plenty of space and withdrawal areas for small groups are all conducive to a good course atmosphere. If possible, participants should be free from all other calls on their time during the course. It is helpful if tea-making facilities are available so that during informal socialising at breaks, course members can relax and shed some of the tensions that may have arisen or share their enthusiasm over new learning.

TIMING AND LENGTH OF COURSE

Experience suggests that courses lasting two to three days have more impact than those consisting of short sessions spread over a number of weeks. There is enough time for rapport to be developed between the leader and participants and among the participants themselves. This gives the course an impetus which is not dispersed in the way it would be if there were a week's gap between sessions. Participants tend to be fresher and therefore more able to learn if a course is held in the daytime rather than in the evenings, tacked on to a day's work. This also applies to leaders. During a full day, breaks every one-and-a-half to two hours are needed.

Ideal conditions may not be possible. If the course is spread over a number of weeks, one-and-a-half to two-hour sessions are probably long enough, especially if held in the evenings when 7.30–9pm seems a useful time. Another aspect of timing to be considered is placement of the course among the other commitments and stresses of participants' lives. If course members are withdrawn from work at a time of seasonal pressure, both they and their fellow-workers may react negatively. Similarly, try to avoid a time when everyone is tired.

MATERIALS

The choice of materials will be determined by the aims of the course, the selection of activities to promote these aims, the amount of money available and the ease of access to facilities for filming or printing, and so on. There can be a temptation to use audio-visual aids to appear up-to-date or novel rather than because they suit your purpose. The key questions in deciding to use audio-visual aids are:

1 What would best suit my purpose?
2 How available are these materials?
3 Am I competent to use them or is technical assistance on hand?

Video and audio tapes are powerful aids in the teaching of counselling skills but they can cause annoyance if the operator is unfamiliar with the equipment or it has not been checked to see if it is working. Sometimes, too, the effort required to obtain and operate these devices is too great to be warranted. The use of audio-visual aids increases rather than diminishes preparation time. Careful planning is required, otherwise the audio-visual aids will be mere gimmicks.

It is helpful to have exercises printed beforehand but they can be presented on overhead projector transparencies, on large sheets of newsprint or on a blackboard. Participants can be asked to bring pens and paper but it is wise to provide some for those who forget. They may also receive directed reading material to use for preparation prior to the course.

LEADERS OF TRAINING COURSES AND WORKSHOPS
A high level of maturity and interpersonal competence is required in those who lead training groups. On the personal level it is desirable that the leader be warm, open, self-accepting, and able to reveal herself. She should be able to refrain from dominating and allow participants to take the initiative. It is important to be flexible and able to change the programme if this is appropriate. The leader needs to be trained, experienced, and proficient in a wide range of skills. Her use of language will be particularly important. It is highly desirable to begin as a sort of apprentice to an experienced leader.

The setting and the composition of the group need to be considered when choosing a leader. Someone who is excellent in an academic setting may not be as effective in communicating to housewives. A high-powered personality may be threatening to those beginning to experience human relationships training for the first time. The leader needs to be someone the group can readily trust and with whom they can feel secure.

Undertaking to train others requires a considerable commitment of preparation time, energy, and involvement. Those who acquire reputations as good leaders need to beware of accepting too many invitations outside their regular jobs because of the demands of intimate forms of communication. A balance of work and leisure is essential.

A leader may come from within one's own organisation or may be invited from outside. An outside leader may not be as threatening in that she does not have to be faced every day after the course is over. Also, an outsider is not already involved in the complexities of colleague relationships with the participants and does not have to worry about facing them afterwards. An inside leader, on the other hand, will be aware of participant characteristics prior to the course; she may have a more accurate assessment of their level of functioning and their needs; and she is more readily available for follow-up, particularly if the training has raised strong anxieties in any group member. These points need to be considered by the organisation when choosing a leader.

EXERCISE 8.1*

You have been asked to run a course for voluntary social workers on Basic Communication Skills. Precisely state your overall aim.

EXERCISE 8.2*

In the course you have chosen to use the following sorts of exercises. What would be your reasons for using each? In other words, what skills would you expect participants to understand, and be able to use after practice?

1 An exercise in paraphrasing (reflecting content). (See pp. 60–61)
2 An exercise in giving feedback as to the accuracy of a partner's listening after she has reflected feeling. (See pp. 60–61)
3 An exercise in sharing feelings. (See exercise 2.4, p. 24)

LEADING GROUPS
The following rules will serve as guidelines for group leaders.

1 Instructions for any exercise or activity should be clear, eg: 'Form groups of three. One group member is to call himself "A", another "B" and the third "C". During the first exercise "A" will counsel "B" with "C" observing.'
2 The leader should beware of dominating or overtalking. If instructions and explanations are clear and concise, a maximum amount of time can be spent on practising the skills.

An example of an explanation of reflecting content follows:
'Reflecting means restating the client's basic message in similar but usually fewer words. It indicates that you have heard and shows how well you have understood. Look at the example you have been given.' (Leader reads this aloud and discusses it.)
'Of course it would be artificial to paraphrase or reflect constantly, but in these exercises you will be asked to do this as a way of focusing on active, accurate listening.'

3 In the small working groups encourage everyone to participate. These hints may help:

(a) Before beginning exercises emphasise that for maximum benefit from the course everyone should participate fully.

(b) Subdivide into pairs or threes. This encourages participation.

(c) Help silent members to participate by occasionally asking them questions. Be aware of their non-verbal reactions and comment when appropriate.

(d) Beware of the person who tries to use the group for his own needs, eg, as an audience. Avoid lengthy monologues or dialogues between one member and the leader by:

   (i) Suggesting that a private issue be discussed at another time, eg, 'As it is a personal matter, I suggest that we discuss this over lunch.'

   (ii) Reminding the group of its purpose for meeting, eg, 'That's interesting but at present we are practising reflecting.'

   (iii) Inviting others to participate, eg, 'Let's hear from Mary now' or, 'What do you think, Mark?'

4 Focus on the here and now rather than on the past or events outside the group.

5 Each person should speak only for himself and not for anyone else or the whole group (unless acting as spokesperson), eg, he should try to say, 'I' rather than 'we' or 'they'.

6 Each person is responsible for the consequences of his or her own actions within the group.

7 As far as possible be aware of each person in the group, not just the current speaker. When leading, look at group members other than the speaker.

8 If people keep directing statements to you as leader, redirect them, eg, 'What do the rest of you think?' or 'What do you think, John?'

9 Be aware of physical movements. They may indicate boredom, frustration, lack of understanding, tension, etc.

10 Accept all feelings without imputing rightness or wrongness to them.
11 Be aware of yourself as a model. As far as possible demonstrate empathy, warmth, and trust.
12 When subgroups are working on exercises, check each group to ensure that members are keeping to the task.
13 If you cannot answer a question, simply say so.
14 Allow the group to decide whether they want the proceedings to be confidential.

Follow-up

For maximum benefit it is valuable to have some form of follow-up. The new learnings are reinforced by subsequent practical work and discussions. Without follow-up the effects of a course may last for only a few weeks while the enthusiasm produced by the course remains.

Follow-up may take the form of one or a series of short meetings. During these, participants may share experiences in using the skills learned, seek support or further direction, or request help in extending their skills. As some courses may gather people from distant places, follow-up via a newsletter, further directed reading, a written sharing of experiences or having district contacts available to answer queries may be helpful. The effectiveness of the course could be assessed by attempting to survey its influence on the subsequent fieldwork of participants.

Another form of follow-up is for participants to report back to their colleagues, or, once they have the experience and confidence, to teach others in their organisations. Again, course members can be made more aware of other, more extended, training courses in their area and encouraged to attend them. Follow-up is vital to strengthen the impact of a course and to stimulate on-going learning.

SAMPLE COURSE

This course is offered as an example.

Basic counselling skills
Purpose
To train teachers to function as deans in a guidance network.
Aims
1 To make the deans aware of the boundaries of their role.
2 To develop active, empathic listening skills.
3 To practise effective responding.

Length
An introductory session of one hour after school followed by two whole days with three sessions per day, each of approximately one-and-a-half hours with breaks for morning tea, lunch, and afternoon tea.
Setting
A school library with carpet tiles and comfortable chairs.
Equipment
Printed handouts.
Four cassette tape-recorders.
Outline
Session 1 A discussion to define the dean's role. The aim was to help deans to recognise their place in the total guidance network, to realise the limits of their role, to assess their strengths and weaknesses and to define their needs for training.
Session 2 Exercises to develop active, empathic listening.
(a) Sentence completion in pairs with the listening partner repeating the speaker's message and asking for feedback as to accuracy. (See Chapter Two exercise 2.4) This was designed to focus on accurate listening with the listening partner providing immediate feedback as to accuracy.
(b) Exercises involving reflection. Participants wrote, spoke, and taped responses to client statements. Again the focus was on accurate listening in which nothing was added or taken away from the essential message. (See Chapter Three pp. 60–61)
Session 3 Identification of feelings from written statements. (See exercise 3.12) The aim was to help deans accurately perceive and respond to expressions of feeling, as this is a significant way of conveying acceptance to a client.
Session 4 Role-playing typical dean-client interviews in pairs before observers, and subsequent discussion. This session was aimed at allowing deans to experience typical dean situations and then critically examine them. They could see various types of interactions and assess their effectiveness.
Section 5 An exercise in listening and response styles. This exercise allowed deans to recognise five types of response (evaluative, interpretative, supportive, probing, understanding), to find out whether they had a particular pattern of responding, and to evaluate the effectiveness of their responses.
Session 6 An examination of responsibilities, resources, and referral. This provided an opportunity to take a detailed look at the dean's place in the total guidance network.
Session 7 A demonstration interview and summing-up. The aims were similar to those in session 4. The summing-up emphasised the need for further training.

9

Developing competence

It is a counsellor's duty to regularly appraise his effectiveness and to take steps towards improving his competence. This chapter suggests ways in which these things can be done.

INTEGRATING THE SKILLS

In progressing through this book counsellors may have felt that it was increasingly difficult to remember and apply everything that had been learned. In addition, they may now feel somewhat unnatural and awkward as they try to implement these skills. It may be reassuring to know that others who have practised similar skills in a problem-solving approach to counselling have reported that training actually seemed to hinder rather than help them at first. These feelings tend to diminish with practice and time. In other words, as a counsellor practises the various skills in real counselling situations, he will begin using them almost automatically and will not be so conscious of his 'performance'. He will begin to develop a personal style that is comfortable, skills-based and problem-oriented.

Trying to focus complete attention on the client is one way of aiding this process. In so doing a counsellor will be more helpful to the client, increase the likelihood of using skills appropriately, and will worry less about what he should be saying or doing. If he can do these things, he will be putting more of his energies into the real purpose of counselling – finding out about, understanding, and helping his client solve her problems.

ESTIMATING PROGRESS

An essential part of counselling is for the counsellor to be able to assess where he is in the process at any given moment. Counselling, after all, is a purposeful activity that follows a predictable sequence. It is important for both counsellor and client to know what progress has been made and what still needs to be done, if only in very general terms. In this book the process has been divided into five stages: (i) defining the client's problem in specific terms; (ii) setting goals for solving the problem; (iii) deciding how to achieve those goals; (iv) implementing a strategy to achieve the goals; (v) evaluating the success of the entire process.

By noting the skills he is using and the types of statements the client is making and by asking himself certain questions, the counsellor can determine where he and the client are in the problem-solving process. The skills discussed in Chapters Three, Four, and Five are divided according to their appropriateness and effectiveness in the various stages of the problem-solving process. Thus, if the counsellor finds himself using mainly defining and clarifying skills and he judges their use to be appropriate at that time in the problem-solving process, he and the client are probably at the first stage of problem-solving, ie, helping the client define and clarify the problem.

The counsellor can also use the client's statements as a guide to progress. For example, client statements of a general, somewhat vague nature ('I'm not really sure – all I know is that I had to talk to someone', and 'Well, what do you think – do I have a problem?') indicate that the process is still at the problem definition stage. Client statements that demonstrate an effort to clarify or specify what they would rather have happen indicate that the process has advanced to the goal setting stage (eg, 'I just want my parents to trust me enough to let me stay out later on weekends.', or 'I need to be able to say what I mean without becoming so nervous and hesitant.').

The counsellor can also determine the present stage of problem-solving by asking himself specific questions. Positive answers to the following indicate that the main task of the stage in question has been accomplished. Negative answers mean that there is still work to be done at that stage before progressing.

Problem Definition
1 Has a problem been identified?
2 Is it stated clearly, in concrete terms?
3 Is it known when and how it occurs?

Goal Setting
1 Does the client know what she would like to do that she cannot do now?
2 Does she know what changes she would like to make? Changes she would like others to make?
Strategy Selection
1 Does the client know how to choose an appropriate goal?
2 Have priorities been established and alternatives evaluated?
Implementation of Strategy
1 Are the implications of the chosen goal and strategy clear?
2 Does the client have the support, resources, and confidence to carry out the strategy?
Evaluation
1 Is the client satisfied with the results of the strategy?
2 Has the original problem been resolved in the desired manner?
3 Is the client able to apply what has been learnt in this instance to future problems?

EVALUATING EFFECTIVENESS

To be an effective counsellor it is essential to assess overall effectiveness. This includes style and its effect on clients, understanding of specific skills and their uses, and success in helping the client solve her problems. It is necessary for the counsellor to make systematic use of a number of sources besides himself in accomplishing this task.

1 He can use a counsellor self-check inventory to assess his own performance. By thinking carefully about what he did and said, he will become more aware of his style and its effect on others.
2 He can have the client complete an interview or counsellor rating scale, in which she is asked to comment both on the interview as a whole and the counsellor's specific behaviour. This will give the counsellor feedback from the 'consumer' on what she found useful, inhibiting, challenging or supporting.
3 Other counsellors could occasionally observe him by sitting in during an interview or by listening to an audio or video recording of the session. Their comments and observations could be an invaluable source of helpful information.
4 The counsellor could join a counsellors' organisation and participate in the business and concerns of that group. By so doing he would become acquainted with others doing similar work, share ideas with them, and think about larger issues facing the helping professions.

SUPERVISION

On-going supervision of practising counsellors is widely recognised as both desirable and essential to the development and maintenance of effective counselling services. For this reason we have described ways in which both supervisors and counsellors receiving supervision can ensure that the process is made more effective.

What is supervision?

While there seems to be general agreement regarding just what supervision is (ie, a learning relationship that enables counsellors to accurately identify their strengths and overcome their limitations in the practice of counselling), there are a number of models for conducting supervision: firstly, supervision as teaching (skills acquisition is the primary goal); secondly, supervision as counselling (personal growth and self-insight are the primary goals); thirdly, supervision as administration (more effective work administration and case management are the primary goals). The fourth model can include aspects of each of the first three. However, its focus is the counsellor's survival in an agency (understanding influence, power, and agency politics are the primary goals). All counsellors, experienced or inexperienced, can benefit from all four types of supervision at varying times.

Who benefits from supervision?

In most instances counsellors perform their services unobserved, in the absence of any accountability checks. Since the quality of these services is of vital importance to the recipients and to the agencies providing them, supervision is one means whereby that quality can be ensured. Supervision also helps to protect the rights and welfare of clients and emphasises the responsibilities of counsellors and agencies to their clients.

More specifically, for *counsellors* supervision serves to foster professional and personal development by extending their knowledge, experience, and skills. It is an intensive learning experience provided in an atmosphere of support and encouragement. Also, since counselling is a stressful occupation in which 'burnout' and infrequent rewards seem to be accepted as inevitable, the use of supervision can provide counsellors with much needed emotional replenishment. Finally, supervision provides counsellors with a means of assessing their job performance. Critical feedback from a supervisor helps the counsellor to explore aspects of his performance.

For *clients*, supervision can function as a quality-control check on the services they receive. Very seldom do clients have an effective, clearly delineated means of participating in the structuring, delivery, or evaluation of counselling services. As recipients they are in an inherently powerless or 'one down' position vis-a-vis the counsellor and the agency. Supervision, if searching and rigorous, will go some way toward ensuring that counselling services are effectively and sensitively provided.

For *agencies*, supervision can result in the provision of better overall counselling services. Administrators will have less need to worry about the performance of counsellors who are receiving competent supervision. For example, counselling can be a highly stressful occupation and supervision can be effective in reducing that stress. It is reasonable for agencies to assume, therefore, that counsellors receiving effective supervision will be less stressed and will be actively engaged in their own professional growth. Hence, they will be better able to cope with the rigours of the job and to develop more effective services generally.

Supervision can also benefit *supervisors*. Providing supervision to other counsellors develops supervisors' awareness of their own personal styles, counselling skills, beliefs and values. The necessity of providing effective supervision to counsellors can also prompt supervisors to identify and overcome their own professional weaknesses, for example, to be more direct, more specific, more problem or task-focussed during supervision itself. Finally, supervision can help to develop a supervisor's self-confidence in undertaking administrative or staff management activities.

Who should supervise?
Supervision will be of greatest benefit when a counsellor selects an experienced, trained counsellor who has had previous experience as a supervisor. It is important that counsellors select supervisors whom they trust and respect and who will challenge them as professionals. Counsellors should avoid asking someone who would have the dual role of supervisor and immediate superior or evaluator. Neither person should be able to use their position or status to influence or manipulate the other.

How does one find a supervisor who will meet one's needs?
It is up to individual counsellors to arrange supervision for themselves by approaching a preferred supervisor and negotiating the practical details of the relationship. One means of locating poten-

tial supervisors is by asking other professional helpers for the names of those counsellors who also act as supervisors. It is necessary as well to ask other helpers for their opinions about supervisors' strengths and weaknesses in the supervisory role and their areas of counselling expertise. Other things to consider include the supervisor's sex, age, race, and theoretical orientation.

Since supervision can be crucial to a counsellor's professional development, counsellors should be confident that the person they ask to be supervisor will be competent to meet their needs. To do this counsellors will need to talk with potential supervisors about their own expectations and the supervisor's beliefs about supervision. Counsellors should determine what they want and need from supervision and be able to express those things clearly. They will also need to decide whether their interpersonal style and personality are compatible with those of the supervisor. Will the relationship be honest, open, and challenging? Counsellors should seek a supervisor who will stay in the role of supervisor for the entire session. Supervision, after all, is for the benefit of the counsellor, and that is where the focus should stay.

Supervisors, too, need to be clear about their beliefs, methods, and orientation regarding supervision. The decision to provide supervision should be made only after a preliminary meeting with and discussion with the counsellor. Finally, it must be remembered that both participants are free to choose with whom they will work, under what conditions, and for how long.

Where should supervision take place?
Ideally, supervision should occur in a neutral, professional setting. This minimises interruptions and phone calls and, hence, serves to emphasise the importance of the supervision process. If supervision must take place in the counsellor's office, efforts should be made to avoid being interrupted, eg, close the door and post a notice asking not to be disturbed. Notify the secretary, if there is one, that no incoming calls will be taken.

How often and how long?
Ideally, supervision should occur every week. If this is not manageable, once a fortnight can still provide benefits. The length of each session should be agreed on by the participants, but it is suggested that 45–60 minutes is both manageable and sufficient. How long the supervision relationship is to be maintained should be negotiated before beginning. For example, both parties may agree to meet initially for four to six months. At the end of that

time they could renegotiate a further term or agree to terminate the relationship. Whatever the agreement, both parties should be clear about the terms at the outset.

How is supervision carried out?
Both counsellors and supervisors must share responsibility for the effective conduct of supervision. Supervisors, for example, should work to ensure that supervision, like counselling, is conducted in as non-threatening, accepting, and understanding an atmosphere as possible. They need to stress that the general goal of any supervision session should be to increase counsellors' knowledge of themselves and their interactions with others. During the course of supervision supervisors can help counsellors to become aware of their specific competencies and weaknesses, and can therefore work with counsellors to enhance or remedy those as the counsellors continue working with their various clients. However, in each particular supervision session it may be useful for supervisors to encourage counsellors to identify specific problems, generate realistic solutions, and implement preferred remedies. The actual structuring of these sessions can parallel the problem-solving approach described earlier in this book. By following such an approach, we believe supervision is more likely to be a productive, learning relationship. Nevertheless, it should be recognised by both the supervisor and the counsellor that the supervisor inevitably has a certain theoretical orientation which will influence the structure and nature of any supervision session.

Counsellors, too, must ensure that their supervision is productive, well-structured, and goal-directed. By reiterating their professional needs, by clarifying their problems and aims in working with clients, and by giving supervisors feedback on the conduct and progress of supervision, they can share the responsibility for its successful conduct.

It is important that counsellors and supervisors do not collude to keep the supervision relationship friendly, polite, and ineffectual so that important and possibly uncomfortable issues are never dealt with. Many such 'games' are possible: 'Let's keep it strictly social.'; 'You be nice to me and I will be nice to you.'; 'Isn't the system awful?'. Supervisors need to be aware of such collusion when it occurs and to discuss it with counsellors directly and openly. One way of doing this is to regularly check that the style and direction of supervision is helpful, relevant to the counsellor's needs, and producing new learning and competencies. For their part, counsellors also need to acknowledge such collusion when it happens and not react defensively or feel overly threatened when it is pointed out to them.

What follows is a list of suggestions for supervisors conducting supervision. The suggestions are not intended to represent an ideal model or procedure, but following them has been found to result in the delivery of more effective supervision, especially by inexperienced supervisors.

1 Begin by asking the counsellor what issues he wants to work on. This should include specific directions regarding what the supervisor should listen for and comment on.

2 Ask the counsellor to give sufficient background information about the topic.

3 Ask the counsellor for a brief, subjective assessment of the case, issue, or work situation.

4 At this point, if using video or audio recordings of a counselling session, play a portion of the tape. Either supervisor or counsellor can stop the tape when wanting to comment.

5 Help the counsellor focus on actual skills used in counselling, aspects of the relationship in question, the overall trend or direction of counselling, basic issues of trust or understanding.

6 Encourage counsellors to evaluate themselves, to make known doubts or ask questions about their own behaviour.

7 Focus on the counsellor's handling of the case rather than becoming mired in the case details. Is there clear evidence of problem-solving activity?

8 Encourage the counsellor to create his own solutions to the dilemmas present in a particular case. It is not the supervisor's role to solve these problems. Rather, the supervisor's role is to act as a consultant to the counsellor (see the section on the counsellor as consultant).

9 At some point during each session, check to make sure that the style and direction of supervision is helpful to and relevant to the counsellor's needs.

10 Terminate each supervision session on a constructive note. Counsellors should be left with clear aims and goals to pursue in their future work.

The above suggestions allow for elements of all four models of supervision: teaching, personal focus, case management, survival in the job. Elements of all four models may be present in the supervision of all counsellors, sometimes in the same session.

Should audio or video tape recordings be used?
While neither is essential to effective supervision, their use enables a more objective and careful examination of what has actually occurred. However, recordings are an aid to supervision, and should not be allowed to become an end in themselves. In fact, the use of recordings can actually introduce problems rather than solve them. For example, it is easy to become overly interested in the details of a case, or to feel restricted to discussing only the contents of a recording, or to feel it necessary to review an entire tape. Finally, it is necessary to obtain a client's prior permission to record all or a portion of any session and to use that recording in supervision.

How is a supervision relationship terminated?
Both the supervisor and counsellor should agree on the length of supervision before the process is actually begun. Both should feel free to terminate the relationship if the needs of either are no longer being adequately met. Too often counsellors can feel trapped in a relationship they no longer find beneficial. They may remain in supervision with a particular supervisor rather than 'hurt the supervisor's feelings' by terminating. Initial contracting can avoid this dilemma. Counsellors should remember that supervision is a legitimately selfish endeavour. It is the counsellor's growth and development that is at stake and competent supervisors accept and understand that fact.

This view of supervision allows for all theoretical orientations. It is not a prescription for the right or only way to conduct and receive effective supervision. However, if counsellors and supervisors follow these suggestions in initiating and conducting supervision, they will notice not only their own respective improvements in confidence and effectiveness, but can also be more confident that clients will receive more effective help.

MANAGING STRESS AND PREVENTING BURNOUT
While effective supervision may help counsellors reduce their work-related stress, the problem is so common and can be so persistent that a more wide-ranging set of coping strategies may be required. A person under stress is characterised by physiological tension and persistent choice conflict, and attempts to reduce such tension often can take a maladaptive form such as illness or work absence (Brammer, 1985). For counsellors, such stress can impair their personal and professional functioning. Symptoms may be psychological (cynicism, emotional exhaustion, feelings of helplessness), physiological (headaches, backaches,

high blood pressure, chronic fatigue, frequent colds and influenza), or behavioural (work absenteeism, social isolation, high job turnover, reduced work efficiency). It is important to realise, however, that (a) different individuals can tolerate different amounts of stress, (b) incidents that are stressful to one individual may be merely motivating or challenging to another, and (c) long lasting periods of stress are generally more harmful than intermittent periods of stress. These must be kept in mind when discussing the effects of stress on counsellors.

Prolonged high stress can result in 'burnout', an end state of work exhaustion or overload (see Cherniss, 1980). The first stage in this progressive loss of job enthusiasm and interest is stress. Therefore, it is imperative that counsellors are alert to signs of stress within themselves and are able to effectively manage and reduce their own levels of stress.

Most stress management courses have focused on strategies to help individuals cope with their own job-related stress, eg, relaxation, physical exercises, meditation, personal time management, hobbies. By comparison, little attention has been paid to organisational or structural stressors. Factors like high case loads, an unpleasant work environment, autocratic and non-participatory administrative procedures, lack of peer support and peer review, role conflict, and role overload may contribute at least as much to a counsellor's job-related stress. Following are suggested methods for coping with or reducing stress in three areas (Edelwich, 1980): personal change strategies; job change strategies; organisational change strategies.

1 Personal change strategies
   (a) exercise regularly;
   (b) develop and maintain close family and social relationships;
   (c) indulge yourself in ways you find pleasurable and relaxing;
   (d) improve your diet and health.
2 Job change strategies
   (a) learn how to manage your work time to your best advantage;
   (b) have realistic work expectations;
   (c) know and accept what the limits of your work responsibilities and your power are and are not;
   (d) extend your skills and understanding through continuing education;
   (e) set achievable, personal work goals;
   (f) get regular supervision;
   (g) achieve a balance between your work and personal life.

3 Organisational change strategies
   (a) try to have case loads (and work generally) reduced;
   (b) seek to improve the working climate of the agency;
   (c) enhance the physical environment;
   (d) work to have administrative procedures made more democratic;
   (e) establish peer support groups;
   (f) ensure that there is regular in-service training available;
   (g) try to ensure that all staff have clear job specifications and know how the organisation works.

CONTINUING YOUR LEARNING

Practising counsellors need to continue their learning and professional development, even after completion of a formal course of training. One obvious way of contributing to such learning is through regular supervision. However, we believe that counsellors should find additional educational and training opportunities to broaden their knowledge, extend their expertise, and keep themselves informed of developments in their own and related fields of helping. Examples of such activities could include:

1 Professional reading (journals, books, monographs);
2 Attending professional conferences, seminars, workshops;
3 Preparing and presenting training sessions for colleagues;
4 Becoming involved in local organisations that are working for change in areas related to your work;
5 Conducting research into problems associated with your clientele;
6 Making a special study of a particular area of your work, eg, aggression, sexual abuse, eating disorders;
7 Writing an article for publication on some topic in which you have a particular interest or expertise.

Answers to exercises

Chapter 3

EXERCISE 3.1

1 (a) Usually the client will feel most comfortable in position 2.

$$\boxed{1\ 00\ 1}$$

   (b) Usually the client will feel that the desk is a barrier between her and the counsellor, but some clients may welcome this distancing. Generally, the most welcoming position is that where both client and counsellor are in front of the desk.

2 Generally, position (b) is the most comfortable for clients.

3 Positions (a)–(c) are usually intimidating, but position (d) is welcoming.

EXERCISE 3.2

All of these situations may be threatening to the counsellor. In each case she first will need to acknowledge the feeings being expressed by the client.

EXERCISE 3.4

(a) 'You seem very upset. Would you like to tell me about it?'
(b) 'I understand you've been made redundant. How do you feel about it?'

(c) 'What would you like to talk about?' or 'How can I help you?'

EXERCISE 3.6

1 (b) and (c) are open-ended.
2 (a) What did you enjoy about the party?
  (b) What caused you to leave school?
  (c) What difficulties are there in getting home?
  (d) How did you come by that jacket?

EXERCISE 3.7

1 You're having difficulty getting a job?
2 You resent this restriction?
3 Can you tell me why?

EXERCISE 3.12

1 (a) Begins with 'I feel . . .' but actually describes what the other person does.
  (b) A strong command, but not a description of a feeling.
  (c) Feeling described is 'anger'.
2 (a) Feeling described is 'depressed'.
  (b) No feeling described.
  (c) 'Anyone' – speaker is not speaking for himself. 'Feels less than his best' is too vague.
3 (a) Describes the reaction but not the specific feeling experienced (ie, was it anger, satisfaction, frustration, etc?).
  (b) Merely asks a question. No feeling is specified.
  (c) The first part is a judgement, the second part describes a feeling – 'mad'.
4 (a) Clearly says 'I'm afraid . . .'
  (b) Begins with 'I feel . . .' but no feeling is specified.
  (c) Loaded with feeling but, again, the speaker's feeling is nowhere described.
5 (a) Makes a judgement about another person and self.
  (b) Does not describe a feeling.
  (c) Feeling described is 'relieved'.
6 (a) Merely describes the exercise.
  (b) Feels 'challenged'.
  (c) Ascribes the feeling 'liked' to everyone, not to self.

Chapter 4

EXERCISE 4.3

1 (a) S; (b) G; (c) G; (d) S; (e) G; (f) G; (g) S; (h) S; (i) G; (j) G; (k) S; (l) S.

Chapter 5

EXERCISE 5.5

Sample Transcript Analysis:

	Skill	Analysis
Teacher 1. The problem is this: I have to teach an intensive French course, to cover a year's work in two terms. I'm doing my best, but I can go only as fast as the students can handle the stuff. And on top of this I have to do all the usual administrative things as well. There's just not time for it all.		(Two issues seem to be emerging: not enough time to do everything and feelings about those demands.)
Counsellor 1. You're feeling, then, that what you're being asked to do is just too unrealistic. Is that it?	Reflection of content plus understanding check.	An attempt to highlight the problem, to focus further discussion.
Teacher 2. Yes. There just isn't enough time. And yet the Principal expects it all to be done. I just think it's impossible. Plus, I don't think she really cares about French.		(Client agrees with reflection and reiterates the problem. The last statement introduces an additional element, possibly feeling laden.)
Counsellor 2. What are your feelings about that, her not caring about French?	Direct, open question.	Directs by focusing on teacher's feelings about Principal's attitude to French.

Chapter 8

EXERCISE 8.1

Overall aim. To develop in participants an increased self-awareness and the skills necessary to meet their clients as people, not problems; to convey trust and warmth, to listen creatively, and to communicate clearly.

EXERCISE 8.2

1 *Paraphrasing:* To enable participants to restate a client's statement in fewer words as an indication of their desire to listen carefully and as a check on the accuracy of their listening.
2 *Giving Feedback:* To teach participants to share their reactions to messages from other people.
3 *Sharing Feelings:* To help participants to identify their own feelings accurately and to share them openly with others.

References

Bowen, M. (1978). *Family Therapy in Clinical Practice*. New York: Aronson.
Brammer, L. (1985). *The Helping Relationship: Process and Skills*. 3rd edn, Englewood Cliffs, NJ: Prentice-Hall.
Cherniss, C. (1980). *Staff Burnout*. London: Sage.
Dixon, D.N. & Glover, J.A. (1984). *Counseling: A Problem-solving Approach*. New York: Wiley.
Edelwich, J. (1980). *Burnout*. New York: Human Sciences Press.
Ivey, A.E., Ivey, M.B., & Simek-Downing, L. (1987). *Counseling and Psychotherapy: Integrating Skills, Theories and Practice*. 2nd edn, Englewood Cliffs, NJ: Prentice-Hall.
Minuchin, S. (1974). *Families and Family Therapy*. Cambridge, MA: Harvard University Press.
Sloane, R.B., Staples, F.R., Cristol, A.H., Yorkston, N.J., & Whipple, K. (1975). *Psychotherapy versus Behavior Therapy*. Cambridge, MA: Harvard University Press.

Select bibliography

COUNSELLING

Brammer, L.M. (1985). *The Helping Relationship: Process and Skills*. 3rd edn, Englewood Cliffs, NJ: Prentice-Hall.

Brammer, L.M. & Shostrom, E.L. (1982). *Therapeutic Psychology: Fundamentals of Counseling and Psychotherapy*. 4th edn, Englewood Cliffs, NJ: Prentice-Hall.

Belkin, G.S. (1981). *Practical Counseling in the Schools*. 2nd edn, Dubuque, IA: Wm C. Brown.

Dixon, D.N. & Glover, J.A. (1984). *Counseling: A Problem-solving Approach*. New York: Wiley.

Donnelly, F. (ed.) (1981). *A Time to Talk*. Auckland, N.Z: George Allen & Unwin.

Egan, G. (1982). *The Skilled Helper: Model, Skills, and Methods for Effective Helping*. 2nd edn, Monterey, CA: Brooks/Cole.

Ivey, A.E. (1988). *Intentional Interviewing and Counseling: Facilitating Client Development*. Pacific Grove, GA: Brooks/Cole.

Ivey, A.E., Ivey, M.B., & Simek-Downing, L. (1987). *Counseling and Psychotherapy: Integrating Skills, Theories, and Practice*. 2nd end, Englewood Cliffs, NJ: Prentice-Hall.

Loughary, J.W. & Ripley, T.M. (1979). *Helping Others Help Themselves: A Guide to Counselling Skills*. New York: McGraw-Hill.

Johnson, D.W. (1981). *Reaching Out*. 2nd edn, Englewood Cliffs, N.J: Prentice-Hall.

Nelson-Jones, R. (1983). *Practical Counselling Skills*. London: Holt, Rinehart and Winston.

Van Hoose, W.H. & Kottier, J.A. (1985). *Ethical and Legal Issues in Counseling and Psychotherapy*. 2nd edn, San Francisco: Josey-Bass.

FAMILY COUNSELLING

Anderson, C.M. & Stewart, S. (1983). *Mastering Resistance: A Practical Guide to Family Therapy*. New York: Guilford Press.

Barker, P. (1986). *Basic Family Therapy*. 2nd edn, London: Collins.

Masson, H.C. & O'Byrne, P. (1984). *Applying Family Therapy*. Oxford: Pergammon Press.

Minuchin, S. (1974). *Families and Family Therapy*. London: Tavistock.

Minuchin, S. & Fishman, H.C. (1981). *Family Therapy Techniques*. Cambridge, MA: Harvard University Press.

Papp, P. (1983) *The Process of Change*. New York: Guilford.

CROSS-CULTURAL COUNSELLING

A. General
Brislin, R.W. (1986) *Intercultural Interactions*. London: Sage.
Gudykunst, W.B. & Young Yun Kim. (1984). *Communicating with Strangers*. Reading, MA: Addison-Wesley.
Marsella, A.J. & Pederson, P.B. (eds.) (1981). *Cross-Cultural Counseling and Psychotherapy*. New York: Pergamon Press.
Metge, J. & Kinloch, P. (1978). *Talking Past Each Other: Problems of Cross-Cultural Communication*. Wellington, NZ: Victoria University Press.
Sue, D.W. (1981). *Counseling the Culturally Different: Theory and Practice*. New York: John Wiley.

B. Māoritanga
Gadd, B. (1976). *Cultural Difference in the Classroom: Special Needs of Maoris in Pakeha Schools*. Auckland, NZ: Heinemann.
Grace, Patricia (1986). *Potiki*. Auckland: Viking.
Heuer, Berys (1974). *Maori Women*. Wellington: Reed.
Hulme, Keri (1985). *The Bone People*. Auckland: Spiral and Hodder and Stoughton.
Ihimaera, Witi (1973). *Tangi*. London: Heinemann.
Jones, Pei Te Hurinui, and Ngata, Apirana Turupa (eds.). (1959). *Nga Moteatea*. Wellington: Polynesian Society.
King, Michael (ed.) (1977). *Te Ao Hurihuri*. Wellington: Hicks Smith and Methuen.
Metge, J. (1986). *In and Out of Touch: Whakamaa in Cross-Cultural Context*. Wellington, NZ: Victoria University Press.
Tuwhare, Hone (1980). *Selected Poems*. Dunedin: John McIndoe.

CONSULTATION
Blake, R.R. & Mouton, J.S. (1976). *Consultation*. Reading, MA: Addison-Wesley.
Boud, D. & McDonald, R. (1981). *Educational Development Through Consultancy*. Guildford, Surrey: Society for Research into Higher Education.
Egan, G. (1985). *Change Agent Skills in Helping and Human Service Settings*. Monterey, CA: Brooks/Cole.
Prebble, T. & Stewart, D. (1981). *School Development: Strategies for Effective Management*. Palmerston North, NZ: Dunmore Press.

SUPERVISION
Boyd, J. (1978). *Counselor Supervision: Approaches, Preparation, Practices*. Muncie, IN: Accelerated Development.
Kadushin, A. (1985). *Supervision in Social Work*. 2nd edn, New York: Columbia University Press.
Powell, D.J. (1980). *Clinical Supervision: Skills for Substance Abuse Counselors: Trainee's Workbook*. New York: Human Sciences Press.